The Power of
Ten Billion Dreams

The Power of
Ten Billion Dreams

by

Ralph S. Marston, Jr.

Image Express, Inc.
Austin, Texas

The Power of Ten Billion Dreams
By Ralph S. Marston, Jr.

Published by:
    Image Express, Inc.
    P.O. Box 66536
    Austin, TX 78766 USA
    Phone 512-401-4900
    Web: www.GreatDay.com

The Daily Motivator® is a Registered Trademark of
    Ralph S. Marston, Jr.

To read The Daily Motivator on the Web,
    visit www.GreatDay.com

For all who dream.

Table of Contents

Your Dream

Nothing happens unless first a dream.
— Carl Sandburg

You have a dream for your life.

Maybe you know precisely what that dream is, or maybe you don't even know it's there. Nonetheless, you have a dream for your life, a vision of experiencing life in a way that is magnificently rich and uniquely fulfilling. Have you seen that dream lately? Or have you been burying it by keeping yourself busy tending to your doubts, your fears and your insecurities? Have you ever allowed yourself to touch the dream you have for your life, to really get to know it?

You are wealthy beyond anything you can imagine.

That wealth is not based on what's in your bank account or stock portfolio, though you can absolutely make use of it to put as much money in the bank as you wish. Your real wealth is not dependent on the make and model of your car, or the size of your house, or on how much stuff you have it filled with. The truly important wealth in your life flows from your own uniqueness. The real richness in your life can be found in the authentic dreams you have for how life can be.

You have a dream that will make your life endlessly fulfilling. Would you like to find it? Would you like to live it?

Maybe you've been thinking about it. Perhaps you've been planning to get around to it, after you lose weight, or as soon as you find a better job, or once you get a little money saved up. Yes, you regret the time you've already wasted but after all, you've been busy just getting by.

Whatever has happened before, is over and done with. Today you have the opportunity to choose how you will move forward. The best option, for yourself and for the whole world, is to live your dreams, beginning immediately. Now you can choose to be who you know, at your deepest and most authentic level, you are meant to be.

Can you feel your purpose? Of course you can. In every like and dislike, in every preference, in every frustration, in every annoyance, in every joy and curiosity and area of interest, in every fascination, are pointers to your purpose. Indeed, you feel it all the time. What does your purpose feel like? It feels like you. It's not who you imagine that other people think you should be. It's who you really are. Your purpose is what you are born to be.

Do you have any brothers or sisters? Are any of them exactly the same as you? Of course not, even though they share your genetics and your upbringing. If those things dictate who you are, then there should be no difference at all between you and your siblings. The fact is, who you are is much more profound than the cells you're made of and the experiences you've been through. Who you are, is you. And what you are meant to do, is live your dream.

That, by the way, is not easy. If you're looking for easy, you can stop right here. If you're looking for someone to give you a secret technique to create happiness and richness without any effort, you won't find it here. There are plenty of people who will promise you that kind of thing, and lots of them will ask you to pay them handsomely for the privilege, but none of them can deliver it to you. Even if they could, you wouldn't want it, not really. Because their pre-packaged vision of happiness, and the things they promise, are not the things that will make you happy. In fact, no *things* will make you happy. You will be happy when you let your *self* be happy. No, that's not a typo. Your self is not quite the same as yourself. Your true self is the part of you that's left when your ego falls away.

If you were told you only had six months to live, your priorities would change drastically. You would completely discard the priorities of your ego. You would live from the perspective of your true self. That true self knows what's really important to you. Your true self knows how to be happy, and it's not by getting things. It's by living your purpose. It's by living your dreams.

But isn't that selfish, to follow your own self-interest? Isn't

The Power of Ten Billion Dreams

it unfair to others when you focus your life around your own dreams?

You feel connected to all that is, and there is great truth in that feeling. From your sense of connectedness comes compassion for others and an appreciation of the whole environment in which you live. Some of your most beautiful desires are your desires to be of service to others and to be a loving, caring steward of the magnificent universe that is your home. Those altruistic desires can make the dreams you carry for your own life seem shallow and selfish by comparison. Be assured, they are not.

On the contrary, it is by following your own unique dreams that you enable and encourage and empower the dreams of others. It is by making purposeful use of the material abundance in the universe that you ensure the sustained viability and integrity of that abundance.

Very likely, the hardest part of living your dreams is making the solid commitment to do so. That commitment hinges on opening yourself to your real, true dreams, and avoiding the temptation to give lip service to the second-hand, superficial, borrowed dreams of others, some of which are not really dreams to begin with. The difficult part is opening up to your dreams. Once you do that, fully and unequivocally, something magical happens. Though in your day-to-day activities there may not even be any noticeable difference, those activities soon begin to yield dramatically different results. What was once tedious, becomes fulfilling. What was once futile, becomes highly effective.

This all depends on you buying into the concept that living your dream is the highest and best use of your life. At this point, you may think that sounds about right. But if you are letting doubt, fear, anxiety or apathy hold you back, then you're not there yet. You'll never be completely fulfilled and satisfied with your life, and that's a beautiful thing. It's a beautiful thing because it always provides you with new ways to make life meaningful. But even though you will never be completely satisfied with where you are, you can be completely satisfied with where you're headed. If that sounds good, keep reading.

Millions of people have found my writing to be helpful. But

the thing is, I don't care whether you like this book or not. I'm not writing it for you, though if my past work is any indication there's a good chance you'll get a lot of great value from it. Here's the truth, though. I'm writing this book for me.

I'm writing it for me because I know that's precisely what will make it the best it can be. And not coincidentally, by doing so I'm illustrating a powerful point, the one I touched on a few paragraphs ago. By following my dreams I'm enabling and encouraging many others to follow their dreams. By following my own dreams, the dreams that resonate with my true self, I'm contributing to life at my highest possible level of effectiveness, and the value of that will go far beyond me.

My biggest, most compelling dream is to live in a world filled with people who live their dreams. This is your invitation to join me there.

The big problem of our age is not massive financial debt. The big problem is not terrorism or greed or tyranny. Those are difficult situations, yet they are mere symptoms of the real problem. The defining problem of our time is not scarcity. On the contrary, it is firmly rooted in overwhelming abundance.

Our big problem is that we think we've become too rich or too sophisticated, too busy or too important, and in many cases way too comfortable, to dream. In our dearth of dreaming we have made ourselves tragically poor. It is a poverty imposed upon each of us not by outside forces but by inner doubts and fears. It is a poverty that is logically unnecessary and yet stubbornly persistent.

There is a way out. It is simple, and yet it can also be enormously difficult. The way forward, the way beyond the biggest problem we face, is to dream. Not a mass, collective dream imposed by an elite group of intellectuals, but a massive collection of individual dreams bubbling up from completely ordinary people with an extraordinary array of perspectives.

The way ahead is for each of us to dream, to really, truly, authentically dream big, meaningful, and outrageous dreams, and then to bring those dreams to life on an entirely personal level. That's the way we've always forged ahead. Now, it is an even more valuable and accessible option. Yet all too often, too many of us are reluctant to make use of it.

Why do we avoid our dreams? The reasons are many, but the reasons don't matter. What matters is that the disregard of dreams is a terminal illness, threatening the very existence of the beautiful and vital body of civilization we've built and nurtured for so long. What truly matter are the very real and unimaginably powerful dreams that live within us, constantly begging and pleading with us to give them light and life.

What do you perceive as the problems in your life? Do you fear you don't have enough of something, like money, or time? Does it seem that the world has passed you by, rendering you irrelevant and virtually alone? Is there some existential challenge, such as a serious health concern or career crisis or dysfunctional relationship that has drained the hope completely out of you? Are you deeply troubled by the constant tectonic churning of political, environmental and economic landscapes?

Whatever manifestation your troubles take, have you ever wondered why they have the power to trouble you in the first place? What is it within you that feels so mortally threatened?

Listen very carefully, and hear the gentle gurgling of a mountain stream. It is early summer, and up above the timberline the snowpack slowly melts, sending a cool, clear, refreshing fount of water coursing over the smooth stones in the stream bed beside you. High in the deep blue sky, the sun casts its brilliance over the whole vista and gently warms your skin. Breathe in the fresh, cool air and listen again, even more carefully. Other than the sound of water in the stream, you hear only peace itself.

Can you imagine such a scene? It feels great to do so. Why does it feel so good? Because you're not just some machine that goes to work and then transports a paycheck to the bank every two weeks. You care deeply about life's beauty. You're not just a piece of meat through which persistent genes provide for their own survival and propagation. You are you. You are awareness itself. You are the beauty and peace that you love so much. You are life experiencing life in a way that it has never been experienced before. In this very moment, through your eyes, the whole universe focuses on its own best possibilities in an entirely unique way.

Your urge to live and to experience is not just some biological or mechanical phenomenon. For at your best, you are a dreamer. The sweet, affirming feeling of fulfillment is the feeling of bringing dreams to life. In the dreaming and living of those dreams is an endless source of magnificent power. You have direct, intimate access to that power.

The real dreams are not those planted in you by clever marketing tactics. Your authentic dreams come from the ineffable substance of who you are. But you are not alone. You live in a world filled with billions of other people who also dream. Though each of those billions of dreams is unique and valuable in its own right, all of them are nonetheless connected. For every dream is made possible by the overriding dream of living a life that matters.

Do you want to change the world? Of course you do. After all, you're alive. And life, by its very definition, is a constant state of change. Because you are alive, you are changing the world all the time. Your desire to live is inseparable from a desire to change the world. For life is change, and meaningful, purposeful change is life. There's even more to it than that. Not only do you change the world by your living presence in it, you have an agenda for doing so. You have within you a vision of how you would like life to be. You have within you a desire to move the reality of your life and your world in the direction of that vision. From that vision, your dreams take shape.

Dreams are difficult. They're not necessarily physically or even mentally difficult, not nearly as much as they used to be. The dreamers who came before us have already figured out most of that stuff. If my great grandfather needed to carry 300 pounds of firewood from one place to another he would have faced a major challenge that might have taken him several days to complete. Today, when I need 300 pounds of compost for the garden I just hop in my Chevy Silverado pickup truck and drive over to Home Depot.

Dreams are no longer physically or mentally difficult. Yet now, dreams are more emotionally difficult. The biggest challenges in following an authentic dream are in clearly knowing what it is and in allowing it to consume your focus. Dreams are extremely demanding. They ask you to open yourself com-

The Power of Ten Billion Dreams

pletely. And that almost always goes against your inclination.

But dreams are crucial. If we don't dream, we begin to fear loss. If we don't dream about what we can create, we fight over the dwindling artifacts from dreams that have already been fulfilled. If we don't dream, our lives run out of value.

Dreams will wake you up at three in the morning, and I'm not referring to nightmares. Dreams are serious, yet they're also a whole lot of fun. And dreams can absolutely change the world, even the little ones.

The Power of Ten Billion Dreams

My Little Dream

*Twenty years from now you will be more disappointed by the
things that you didn't do than by the ones you did do. So throw
off the bowlines. Sail away from the safe harbor. Catch the
trade winds in your sails. Explore. Dream. Discover.*
— Mark Twain

On the Caribbean island of Barbados is a wonderful place
called the Waterfront Café. It's a restaurant that sits right on
the Careenage, which is a marina filled with beautiful yachts
in the middle of the capital city of Bridgetown. In addition
to delightful seafood and other Caribbean dishes, inside the
Waterfront Café you'll find live jazz music on most evenings.
Or you may choose to sit at a table outside, and enjoy a view of
the Barbados parliament building and clock tower across the
small harbor.

I have a dream of traveling to the Waterfront Café, to sip a
mojito while enjoying Bajan fish cakes and shrimp in coconut
curry sauce, with a live jazz band setting the mood. But the
substance of my dream is not really about having dinner at a
particular restaurant, as delightful as that may be. My dream
is all about how I will get there. Because not only do I intend
to dine at the Waterfront Café in Barbados, I intend to request
a table outside so I can keep an eye on a boat in the harbor.
My boat. A sailing yacht. The one I will sail there from Corpus
Christi, Texas.

It is not the being there in Barbados that makes up the
substance of my dream. It is the getting there. I've loved to
sail since before I was in college. I've loved traveling to the islands of the Caribbean almost as long. Some of the best days
I've ever experienced were spent sailing in the Caribbean and
elsewhere. I've never undertaken a sailing journey that's anywhere near this ambitious, but I've always fantasized about
it. Now that fantasy has been crystallized into a very specific
dream. It feels completely right. It feels powerful. In fact, it
feels so powerful that it has given me a whole new apprecia-

tion for the power of dreams.

And that's what this book is about—the power of dreams. Just one single dream can be immensely powerful. In fact, just one dream can change the world. But the thing is, I don't have just one dream. My dream of sailing from Corpus Christi to Barbados is a relatively small dream. That's why I refer to it here as my little dream. Yet even a little dream has the power to change the world, as we shall explore in these pages. That's because dreams do not exist in a vacuum. They build upon and interact with other dreams, and the resulting synergy moves all of life forward. I have my little dream plus many others. You have dreams, too, and so does everybody else. In those dreams, in the combined power of all those unique, personal, individual dreams, is the power to move life to a higher level for every person in the world—the power of ten billion dreams.

Perhaps you find my little dream interesting, or perhaps you don't. Maybe you're so captivated by it that you beg me to bring you along. Or, you may think it is entirely frivolous and a waste of time. Perhaps you've sailed a small boat all the way across the Pacific Ocean and you consider my plans of merely traversing the Gulf of Mexico and hopping through the Lesser Antilles to be no big deal. Or maybe you've never even seen the ocean and it's difficult for you to imagine going across it, not to mention in a small boat. Yet whatever you may think of my dream, it is indeed my dream (one of many), and it is authentic. It is something that I am passionate about and that I fully intend to accomplish because of the way I know the experience will make me feel, and because of the way it already makes me feel even though I have not completed it yet.

And whether you resonate with my dream or not, it has value to you. Even if you think that my dream is completely frivolous and hopelessly self-serving, it still has value to you and to a whole lot of other people. Because the value that I create in the process of achieving that dream will go far, far beyond me and my little dream. A significant part of that value you are holding in your hands right now, for this book is a direct result of my dream of sailing to Barbados.

For a long time I've been meaning to write another book. My previous book was published almost six years ago. And although I had done a lot of writing on another book since that time, it was lacking something. There was nothing to tie it all together. Then one cool fall evening, I wanted to sit outside and read a book in the new lawn chair my wife had given me. So I went to the bookshelf intending to get an old favorite book about economics. But another book caught my eye, a book about long sea voyages in small boats. Years ago I had been a member of a sailing book club, and that particular book had been one of the monthly selections. I had never read it, so I decided that night it was about time to do so.

Sitting out on the deck in the cool night air, I began to re-acquaint myself with my passion for sailing. The more I read about the adventures of others, the more I wanted to be out on the ocean myself. I began to think about my own sailing adventures, most of which were long ago, before life was so complicated and busy. And then it hit me. It was time to go sailing again, and not really for the enjoyment of it but for the challenge and the sense of accomplishment. Well, ok, for the enjoyment too! I immediately thought about Barbados. It's a beautiful place, and there's something there that resonates with my spirit. It's a place where I love to spend time. And it's far enough away to present a real and exhilarating challenge. Suddenly, the dream was born. A sailing adventure from Texas to Barbados! The more I thought about it, the more I realized it was meant to be. But I didn't just realize it on an intellectual level. I felt it, and that feeling has been growing ever since. Now, more than ever, I feel it is meant to be and I am already working diligently to bring it about.

But formulating my dream was just the beginning. The next day, on my morning walk, I was thinking about that freshly-minted dream. In particular, I was thinking about how quickly and powerfully it had energized me, and improved my whole attitude toward life. I was literally feeling the immense power of an authentic dream growing within me, the power of my own dream. I knew without a doubt that it was real, and I knew without a doubt that I would make it happen. And then I had another epiphany. I realized what I was doing. Dreams—the power of dreams! That's what would tie my book together! Without fully understanding it over the last few years, that was precisely the theme of what I had been writing about in all the writing I had done for the book.

Although I feel tremendously blessed to have already achieved many dreams in my life, the dream I've chosen to share in this book is one that has not yet been fully realized. The value of a dream begins the moment you first feel it, and it can grow steadily each day until the dream is realized. The dream of sailing my own boat to Barbados already has given my life incredible new energy, and I have only just begun to work on it. By sharing that fresh, new dream and by expressing its energy through the words in this book, my intention is to inspire you to jump right into your very own dreams, right now, and to immediately begin experiencing the benefits of their positive power.

There are so very many problems in our world today, to the extent that they seem absolutely overwhelming most of the time. All sorts of well-meaning people dedicate themselves to solving those problems, and yet it seems to be a Sisyphean task. The solution to one problem creates other problems, and still other problems grow more onerous at the same time.

But there is something much stronger than the power of a problem, and that is the power of a dream. Throughout the ages, dreams built upon dreams have lifted us so high that we're in the fortunate position of not even realizing how good we have it. Yes, there are problems, but most of those problems are just plain trivial when compared to the challenges faced by the first humans. Our ancestors faced mortal challenges on a daily basis. Many of them spent nearly every moment in the survival mode. Even so, some of them had a little bit of time and energy to dream. Some of them acted on their dreams, and made a little bit of progress. Generation after generation of successive dreaming has brought us from dreaming of a warm place to spend the night to the point where we can now dream about such things as crossing the ocean in a sailing yacht or even flying into outer space. There is no limit to the power of dreams.

However, there are very real limitations that do prevent dreams from being realized. Those are the limitations we put on our own dreams, both individually and collectively. All too

The Power of Ten Billion Dreams

often, we tend to discount our dreams or ignore them altogether. And when that happens, a negative momentum takes hold and the richness of life begins to fade away.

If you're driving your car, and it is running very low on gas, and there's a gas station up ahead, what do you do? That's easy—you pull into the gas station and fill up your tank, of course. You'd be crazy to speed on past the gas station. Ignoring your dreams is like driving on past that gas station, even as the "low fuel" warning chime is sounding in your ears. Without a meaningful and compelling dream, life quickly runs out of energy. That happens not only on an individual basis, but throughout society. It's when people stop dreaming that the problems start arising.

Are the passion and energy in your life in fact running low right now? Are you perhaps feeling tired of the drudgery of just getting by? Are you tired of having to make do with the limited options that are available to you each day? Or have you actually gone past being tired, to the point where you're really fearful about the fact that your life seems to be going nowhere? Are you aching to feel fulfillment, not just every now and then, but in every single moment, on every day of your life? Do you wish to feel that sweet sense that all is right with life, no matter where you are and what you are doing?

Have you had enough of making compromises? Are you fed up with being frustrated by the foolishness and incompetence you encounter in the world around you? Do you want to be able to do work that is meaningful and rewarding? Are you weary from being frightened, from all your worrying about what tomorrow will bring? Are you sick of the anxiety that comes from living in a world where so many of the things that affect you are out of your control? Are you tired of feeling irrelevant, and confused by the complexity of life?

Are you ready to truly live, to see life's beauty in every direction? Are you ready to take action and to get real, meaningful, valuable, rewarding results from that action?

Then it's time for you to dream, and to truly live that dream. It's time to reach deep within yourself and grab a big handful of real, authentic purpose, and use that purpose to fashion an irrepressible dream for yourself. What's most important is that the dream is truly yours, something that, once you realize what it is, you absolutely know you cannot be without it. It doesn't matter if other people see that dream as silly, or worthless, or selfish, or too ambitious, or not ambitious enough, or whatever. What really counts is that it is authentically yours. What really counts is that it is something you truly want to do.

Many people see dreams as frivolous, particularly in times of economic uncertainty. That makes sense of course, and is very logical reasoning. But in fact, the truth is the other way around. In difficult times, dreams are more important than ever. A lot of people see dreams as selfish, and think that it is much more compassionate to focus on helping others than it is to focus on one's own dreams. That's completely reasonable and understandable. After all, compassion is a beautiful thing and is essential to our civilization. Within each of us is an impulse to help others, and we can all be much more successful when working together than when fighting against each other. Yet if you wish to be compassionate, what is the best way to do that? If you ignore and deny your own dreams, does that put you in a better position to be of service to others? Actually, as we will discover, it doesn't. Because in order to give of yourself to others, you must have something to give. It is through living your dreams, whatever they may be, that you create real value in your life and in your world, value that you can offer to others in great abundance. If, on the other hand, you suppress your own dreams in the interest of helping others, all you're doing is reducing the amount of value that you have to work with. Nobody benefits from that. In fact, it hurts us all.

I readily admit that my dream of sailing to Barbados is highly self-serving. After all, it involves sailing through the beautiful, warm islands of the Caribbean and generally having a very good time at it. On the surface, it would seem that a more responsible and compassionate dream would be to provide loving foster homes for troubled youth, or to provide clean water to villagers in Africa, or mosquito nets to people in areas prone to malaria. These are great causes, by the way, and I'm happy to be able to support them along with other good causes. Plus, I do have other dreams that are not so

The Power of Ten Billion Dreams

blatantly self-serving as my dream to sail to Barbados. One of those dreams is a passionate desire to encourage others to dream, which is what I seek to do with this book. Yet I have chosen to share my sailing dream with you precisely because it is not a "save-the-world" type of dream, precisely because it appears, on the surface, to be so self-serving. My intention is to illustrate a powerful point. It's a point that, when you truly get it, can profoundly change your life and can in fact enable you to change the whole world for the better. By introducing you to my little dream, and by considering all the wonderful and valuable things that dream sets in motion, I intend to install within you a beautiful and powerful certainty, which is this:

Any dream, as long as it is positive and authentic, serves to move the whole world forward. Even if the dream is not, on the surface, about doing good things for others, it will nevertheless end up being of great value to all.

I know that may be difficult to believe. I completely understand if you have doubts. My job is to erase those doubts. My job is not merely to get you to believe the statement above, but to get you to the point where you know it without even the possibility of doubt, where you don't have to take my word for it. My purpose, with this book, is to set you free to dream, so that the immense value within you is expressed in ways that benefit the whole world.

Each person in this world is a unique individual, with his or her own special set of desires and dreams. The world desperately cries out for all those dreams and the creative, productive power they can inspire. Unfortunately, far too many dreams have been destroyed by self-criticism or by the judgments of others. And when that happens, real, authentic dreams can be replaced by borrowed dreams, or worse. Those borrowed dreams are just cheap imitations, though, and they have no power to move life forward. It is not my place, and not the place of anyone else, to pass judgment on anyone's dreams. Your dreams, when they are sincere, positive and authentic, do not ever have to conflict with the dreams of others. And in living your authentic dreams, whatever they may be, you do a great service to all that is. In fact, the truth is that you owe it to life to dream.

The Power of Ten Billion Dreams

Barbados is a long way from Texas. My route will take me around the arc of the US Gulf Coast to Key West, through parts of the Bahamas and then to Puerto Rico, from where I will island hop south past St. Lucia, and then eastward to Barbados. It's a total distance of more than 3,000 miles, with many stops along the way. Some of those stops will be in places I already know and love, and others will offer completely new adventures. Though I am a long way from actually setting sail on this journey, I have already begun to start to make it happen. That's an important thing to realize about dreams. The value begins to flow long before a dream is fully reached. In fact, it's really more appropriate to speak of dreams as unfolding than to refer to them as being reached. That unfolding begins the moment your dreams are born, and continues to benefit the whole world as you continue to focus on those dreams and bring them to life. Are you ready to feel the power of living your dreams? Then let's move forward.

Achievement Machine

That some achieve great success, is proof to all that others can achieve it as well.

— Abraham Lincoln

What if you had a machine that could produce anything you could imagine—any object, no matter how complicated, any experience, no matter what it involved, any relationship, any feeling, any circumstance, any situation that you could imagine, any organization, any group of people you could imagine, any visual thing you could imagine, any sound you could imagine. Just think of how it would be to have such a machine, that could literally create anything. Aside from the fact that it would be absolutely amazing, what would it be like in a practical sense?

To start with, it would need to be very flexible. It would have to be able to accommodate whatever you asked of it, whatever you ordered from it. It would have to be flexible in another way, too. It would need to be able to adapt to changing conditions. Plus, it would have to be reliable and predictable. If you had such a machine, you would definitely need to have confidence in it. You would want to be assured that every time you supplied it with a vision from your imagination, it would faithfully, dependably and precisely bring whatever you envisioned into reality. With such a powerful machine, you wouldn't want it to get things wrong.

If you had a machine like that available to you, a machine that could produce whatever you told it to produce, what kinds of things would you dare to dream? Keep in mind that we're not talking about anything magical here—just very, very advanced and very powerful. The machine would most certainly operate within the confines of physical reality and adhere to the laws of physics. As such, it would require energy. It would require maintenance. It would require support in order to keep running. It would have to be supplied with raw materials.

But most of all, it would need to be accurately instructed

about what it was you wanted it to do. You would have to be able to tell the machine, in no uncertain terms, very precisely, very specifically, in complete detail, exactly what you expected it to produce. And then, you would have to learn how to operate it. It would not be easy. It would not be simple. There would be some complexity to operating this machine. Because after all, it would be an enormously complex and flexible and productive and powerful machine. And you couldn't just let it run wild. With power comes the responsibility to learn how to use that power in a reasonable, wise and benign way that would not harm you or others.

So that's what the machine would look like. And there's one main thing it would need to have in order to operate—it could have all the other stuff and yet if it did not have this one essential thing it would not do any good. What would that be? The machine would need to know what you wanted it to produce. It would need to know the kinds of situations you wanted it to create. It would need to know the kinds of objects and product and things and stuff, materials and fuels and whatever, it would need to know the specific physical objects you would want to create. It would need to know the experiences you would want to create with it. It would need to know the sights, the sounds, the tastes, the feelings of what you wanted to get from it.

Without an input, this machine would not do anything. It would be fabulous in its complexity, amazing in its power, incredible in its scope and ability to create literally anything that you could think of, and yet, the key words there are "think of". The key thing about using this machine would be to imagine, to give it a meaningful objective to work with. Because this machine would work, but it would work best when fulfilling authentic desires.

What if you had access to such a machine? What would you ask of it? What would be your input? What would you get the machine to produce for you? And just as importantly, why? Why would you ask it for the things you would ask it for?

Would you, for example, just ask it for frivolous things, any old thing that popped into your head? Imagine what would happen if you did that. Before long, your life would be filled with those trivial things, those trivial things that popped into your head. They would fill your life. They would be everywhere. You would have so much stuff in your life—not just physical stuff, but relationships, situations, experiences—that really didn't mean anything. They just might have happened to sound good at the time you asked the machine for them. And then the moment you envisioned them, the machine went to work and made them. It would have put them in your life, and then you'd have been stuck with them.

Would you really want that? It would be an enormous burden on your life to have to carry around all that stuff with you, to have to figure out where to put it and what to do with it. So you don't want the machine to produce just anything you tell it on a whim. What you want the machine to produce are only the things that are truly meaningful to you. You wouldn't want to waste all that time and effort and capability of this fantastic machine on stuff that doesn't really matter. It would be much better to use the machine to create a life that is stunningly fulfilling, a life that is amazing, a life that is outstanding, full of wonderful people, enriching experiences and places to go, sounds, sights, tastes, aromas, things really turn you on, that you love, things that make you feel vibrantly alive. Those are the kinds of things you'd use the machine to create.

The amazing thing is, there is such a machine. In fact, right now, you are literally surrounded by the greatest achievement machine the world has ever known. With little more than an idea and the commitment to make that idea into something valuable, you can take the controls. And you can effectively utilize this achievement machine to begin manifesting your idea into reality. It's not magic. It's the result of centuries of exploration, learning, discovery, and progress in the fields of science, philosophy, literature, communication, technology, industry, transportation, law, organization, management and other disciplines far too numerous to mention. You have at your beck and call a whole host of amazing technologies, capabilities and resources, most of which would have been unimaginable just a couple of hundred years ago, many of which would have been unimaginable just a few decades ago. And not only you, but a growing number of other people all over the world have access to the grand achievement machine that is present-day civilization.

You can take the controls of a small little aspect of it and you can put your desires into it, you can put your wishes into it, and by knowing what to do, by knowing how to pull the right levers, and say the right words, and do the right things, you can make stuff happen. You can successfully operate this machine. It's a living machine. It consists of every other person on the planet.

If you can imagine something, there is a way for you to achieve it by tapping into the power of the amazing worldwide achievement machine. Yes, it will require much effort and commitment on your part. Yes, it will take time. But as long as you're going to be spending time anyway, you might as well be working toward bringing your most treasured dreams to life. There is nothing more fulfilling than spending your time and effort in the service of what you are most passionate about. And the amazing, worldwide achievement machine offers more possibilities for doing that than ever before in history.

This is a major deal. It used to be that in order to manufacture a product, you needed a factory. You needed enormous amounts of capital and a well-trained labor force. Now, all you need is a computer and an Internet connection. With that, you can find a manufacturing plant somewhere in the world that will make your product in any quantity you require.

This book is a good example. Years ago when I published my first book, it was self published. That in itself was something that had not been practical for very long. Using layout software on my desktop computer, I created the camera-ready original of the book. Then I found a printing company to print the book. The only catch was that I had to pay several thousand dollars to get the minimum quantity printed. That was about 12 years ago. Now, with this book, I will simply upload a computer file and the book will be printed on demand, as orders are received for it. Unlike the earlier books, I won't have to have a minimum of 1,000 copies printed at a time, and I won't have to find a place to keep all that inventory. When an order is received for the book, one copy will be printed and shipped to the customer.

The Power of Ten Billion Dreams

A similar thing has occurred in the music industry. The large, powerful music publishing companies of the past are quickly becoming irrelevant. Artists can now produce and distribute their own recorded music, cutting out layers of middlemen. They can sell their songs for a lower price while making more money on each one sold. The same thing is happening in just about any field of endeavor.

Never before in history have so many people had so much access to such powerful capabilities. Imagine this. There is some particular thing you need that's sitting in a warehouse on the other side of the world. Perhaps it's a replacement cooling fan for your computer. With just a few taps on your smartphone, you can command armies of workers to locate the part, package it, and ship it thousands of miles so that it is sitting on your front doorstep the next day. And you don't need to pay a king's ransom for the privilege. It's commonplace. It's done all the time. When you consider what's actually happening, it is amazingly affordable. Or what if you want to know the average temperature in February in Riga, Latvia? The information is just a few mouse clicks away, as is just about any other fact you might want to know.

The amazing worldwide achievement machine can take you to anywhere you wish to go, can deliver to you anything you would like to have, can connect you with other people who share your interests as well as those who disagree with you, no matter how far away and how widely scattered they may be, and can provide you with an endless variety of entertainment experiences, as well as more information than you could ever digest in a lifetime. It can provide you a vast array of financial and investment options. It can nourish your body with all sorts of exotic foods and beverages, and provide you with medicines to heal your illnesses, and the experts to administer them. It can enable you to do, to be, or to create pretty much anything you can imagine. Are you getting all this?

So what exactly is this achievement machine? It is human civilization itself. Our present day civilization has been built upon achievement, and it enables great achievement, much greater levels of achievement than would be possible without it, by orders of magnitude. What makes it so powerful and effective is a very basic, yet powerful concept. Underlying the amazing worldwide achievement machine is the understanding that it is better for us to respect and cooperate with each other than it is for us to fight against each other. What makes it work is that there are so many people who are willing to offer one kind of value in exchange for another kind of value. And that is precisely how you tap into the power of the amazing worldwide achievement machine. You find a way to offer real, unique value. Somewhere, there are people who wish to bring that very value into their lives, and they are willing to provide value of their own in order to have it.

The amazing worldwide achievement machine is built on dreams. It is sustained by dreams. And by tapping into its power, you can fulfill your own dreams, whatever they may be.

For the fulfillment of my own dream, I will require a lot of things. First and foremost, I must have a sailboat. I will also need to become more skilled at sailing and navigating in the open ocean. I will have to have fuel, water, ice and other provisions, and those things must be re-stocked along the way. I will need to have good communication capabilities, so I can continue publishing *The Daily Motivator* each day during the trip. I will need places to moor and dock the boat along the way, and perhaps occasional transportation back home during the course of the trip. I will have to have many, many more products and services than I have even thought about yet. On top of all that, the adventure will require an enormous amount of specialized information. I am confident that the amazing worldwide achievement machine can provide me with all those things. In fact, it has already begun to do so.

I also know that in order to acquire those things, I will need to exchange something of value for each one of them. So, in order to live my dream of sailing to Barbados, I will have to create new value to offer to the world, new value in the form of books such as this one, more daily inspirational messages, audio programs, and other things that I'm skilled at creating. That's how the achievement machine works. I create value and exchange that value for other value, and in the process, even more value is created. It is a wonderful dynamic, and it is ready and waiting to fulfill every dream that can be imagined.

The Power of Ten Billion Dreams

One truly great thing about the amazing worldwide achievement machine is that I can do what I do best, and create the kind of value that I'm skilled at creating, and then I can exchange that value for the other kinds of value that I require and desire. This makes me infinitely more effective and productive.

If, for example, I had to grow all my own food, build and maintain my own housing, transport myself from place to place by my own devices, and do a whole host of other tasks necessary for daily life, I would have no time left to do anything else. As it is, the worldwide achievement machine takes care of my daily needs. Yes, I pay money for those things but I have enough money because I'm able to create my own unique value and to get paid for it. The system works amazingly well. It works so well, in fact, that we take it for granted. It is so ingrained and dependable that we don't even think about what's going on.

The fact is, though, that thousands, even millions of people around the world are involved in supplying you with the things you make use of on a daily basis—fresh oranges and bananas, electricity, water, tequila, flashlight batteries, gasoline for your car, vitamins, a pen to write with, blank DVDs, wireless telephone service, and countless other things. Imagine trying to create just one of those things yourself. Imagine, for example, building a AA battery. Would you have any idea where to begin? Yet you can buy a package of 20 of them for six dollars.

The real question is, why does all this happen? Why is all this amazing stuff so readily available? The answer? Dreams. You can buy AA batteries because somebody had a dream to build a factory to manufacture those batteries. That person, and all the people who work in the factory, as well as the people who supply the factory, are being paid to provide you with the AA batteries you require. All because of the power of dreams.

Think of it. We live in a world filled with people who have the power to dream, and who are robustly connected to each other. Many of those connections are in ways we know about. We're connected by the Internet, we're connected by telephones, we're connected physically, we're connected by trains and ships and airplanes and automobiles, that are able to transport us from one place to the next so we can meet in person with each other. We're connected by language. We're connected by art, by common experience. We're connected by Fedex and UPS.

In addition, we're connected in ways we don't know about, in ways we don't yet realize. There are connections between us that we may not even know about, but still they exist and still they exert their influence. And I'm not talking about magical, mystical things. I'm talking about real things that we just don't fully understand yet. It's a complicated world. Suffice to say, though, that we are thoroughly and intractably connected to each other.

Because of that, we can do powerful and amazing things for each other to support each other's dreams. In addition to us being connected to each other, the vast majority of people have the sense that we're all in this together, and that what's good for everyone else is good for me, and vice versa, what's good for me is good for everyone else.

Sure, there are situations when one person is technically the winner and others are not. In a footrace, for example, there's one person who is the winner and the other participants don't win. But every person in the race has the positive experience of participating, if they choose to see it that way. When two teams meet on a field, one wins and the other doesn't, but that's a game, and we play it because we want to play in a game.

In the business of following positive, authentic dreams, though, when one person wins, many others also win. Imagine fifteen people stuck on an island somewhere, and one person figures out how to grow a garden. That person wins, and everyone else wins too, even if that person makes everyone else pay him for the food from his garden by perhaps asking them to haul water or catch fish. Everyone wins because the fruits of that garden are available to the people on that island. Yes, it might cost them something to get it (and really it's better if it does, as we'll discuss later) but that's ok. They still win. They're still better off than they would be if the fruits and vegetables were not there. They have access to them.

And so in the same way, if someone figures out how to take oil out of the ground and refine it, even though that person charges other people for the oil and the fuel it produces, still everybody is better off because that one person, or in the case of oil, that large group of people who form an oil company, are able to get that oil out of the ground and refine it into fuel that people can use. Even though the oil company charges people for it, even though they may in fact charge extremely high prices for it, people are better off because of it. Why? Because the fuel that is produced has great value. It warms people's homes, it transports them from place to place, it enables them to fly through the air. Think of that—what an amazing accomplishment it is for people to reliably travel by air, and it's something we mostly just take for granted. Without oil, and the fuel that's made from that oil, air travel would simply not be feasible with our current technology. Some people get very rich from finding and producing that oil. Yet their wealth pales in comparison to the enormous positive value that people all over the world receive from having access to the powerful fuels that come from that oil.

So, we're all connected, and when one person truly wins in an authentic way, when one person creates value, that cannot help but benefit everyone else. It is a situation ripe with opportunity for those who make the choice to follow their dreams. Our robust connections provide us with ample opportunities to create value and to exchange that value for other value, thereby making even more value.

We have this amazing machine. And the machine is working all the time, all around the world. We're all connected to it. We can all access it in our own ways. Some people have figured out how to get high bandwidth access to it, and they can create a great amount of value. Most of those people have worked long and hard to get themselves into such a position, where they can make valuable, effective and efficient use of the amazing worldwide achievement machine. In some places it works better than others, in some situations it doesn't work as well as in other situations. But the thing is, it works. And we're all connected to it. And we all have the potential to benefit from it in ways that are personally meaningful.

Some people have greater access. Others don't have quite as much. One big problem is that many people don't realize it exists. It's hiding in plain sight. People see all the factories and transportation and communication networks, but they fail to realize how easily accessible most of them are. They fail to fully realize the implications of being able to interact with so many people. Many people don't look beyond their own narrow concerns, and think that "somebody else" is in charge of making and distributing all the valuable and useful products and services they use on a daily basis. In fact, no one is really in charge. That's the amazing thing. The enormous value that's produced in our world is not produced under the auspices of any kind of grand, centralized authority. It comes from people who are motivated to act in their own interest, and by so doing, their efforts yield value for many, many others. Yet there are lots of people who don't see it that way. When those people look only at their own narrow concerns, the world looks very unfair to them.

Well, the world is unfair. Life is unfair. Very unfair. We're not born with a lot of advantages. We have to make our own way in life. That's been the case forever. But we have the tools, individually, to do that, to make our way successfully through life. And the thing is, the situation has greatly improved. Over the last few thousand years, we've increasingly connected ourselves with other people, building what is now our highly interconnected civilization. We've come to the realization, individually and collectively, that we're better off working together, that we can get a lot more stuff done when we work together. When we coordinate with each other, when we cooperate with each other, we can create much more value than if we just worked individually. There are things that it is just impossible to do as an individual, but which can be done with enough people working together who have mutually beneficial interests.

The point is that we are connected and we have achieved great success by understanding and utilizing the value of those connections. The most successful among us realize the value of being connected to each other, and of the things we can do in cooperation with each other. And so it all combines togeth-

The Power of Ten Billion Dreams

er to create a vast, amazing worldwide achievement machine. You can feed your dreams into this machine, and by operating the machine in a certain specific way, you can bring those dreams to life.

Though I refer to it as a machine, I most assuredly don't mean to objectify the people who make up this machine. Each person is an individual, and that's the point. The amazing worldwide achievement machine is made up of individual people, each with his or her own perspective, with his or her own unique skills, abilities and opinions, understanding the benefits of working cooperatively with other people. Each person can find a rewarding place in the machine. In the best possible scenario, each person settles on what he or she does best, all doing what they each prefer to do, doing what they can do competently and effectively, and making the machine work.

But by no means is each person merely a cog in the machine, though that's kind of how we've pictured it for the last few hundred years. At one time that characterization was fairly accurate. Since the dawn of the industrial revolution a lot of the work has been largely menial and tedious, but still it has still has been fulfilling in the sense that it has enabled vast numbers of people to raise their standards of living significantly. It hasn't been perfect by any means. There have been great difficulties and pains, and yet the rewards have been even greater.

We have now reached the point where the amazing worldwide achievement machine has evolved to a higher level, with much greater empowerment for individuals. This is an outstanding time to connect with your dreams, and to bring them to life. Never before in history have so many people been so powerfully empowered to live their unique, authentic dreams. Are you ready to begin living yours?

The Power of Ten Billion Dreams

Your Great Opportunity

Hell begins on the day when God grants us a clear vision of all that we might have achieved, of all the gifts which we have wasted, of all that we might have done which we did not do.
— Gian Carlo Menotti

So what does all this mean to you? With more opportunity for meaningful individual achievement than ever before, how do you make the most of it? What does it take to access and create value from the amazing worldwide achievement machine?

What's absolutely necessary is a dream. You've got to have a dream that will push you forward. You've got to have a purpose that is meaningful to you, a purpose so compelling it will keep you up at night. And you must come up with a very specific, detailed expression of that purpose, something you can articulate to yourself and others in a compelling, inspiring way. It is that purpose that will have to keep you going through the most difficult times, and be powerful enough to keep you inspired in spite of all the challenges and obstacles and disappointment and pain. The expression of your purpose must be strong enough and meaningful enough to keep you putting forth persistent effort over the long haul. Plus, it must provide you with specific, achievable objectives that you can work on reaching in a disciplined, focused way.

What? You say you're not disciplined or focused enough to do that? Of course you are. If you've never experienced a high level of discipline or focus in your work, it's just because you've never worked on something that means the whole world to you. When you're working on a real, authentic dream, you'll be amazed to find plenty of discipline, plenty of focus, and plenty of whatever else you need to get the job done. We often think of discipline as something that has to be enforced from outside of us. But the best kind of discipline is the discipline you enforce on yourself. That's the kind of discipline that comes naturally and abundantly to you when you're living your dream.

A dream is really all about the way you want to feel. Because the objects, the material stuff that you get from your dream, the places you go, the people you associate with, the experiences you have—those all contribute to a feeling that you desire to have. You want to feel fulfilled, certainly, but you wish to feel your fulfillment in a specific way, in a way that's yours and yours alone, in a way that is your unique expression of what it is to be alive. That's what you long to manifest in the world. That's what you desire to express. That is the essence of your dream.

So although your dream might be to sail to Barbados, the sailing to Barbados is only the expression of the dream. The real, fundamental, invisible aspect of your dream is how you will feel when you're living it. The dream of owning a home in the mountains is not, at its root, about the home itself. The dream is about the way you'll feel when you are living in that home. For this reason, it is not possible to borrow someone else's dream. If you try to do that, all you get is a token of the dream, not the fulfillment of the dream itself. The dreams that will pull your life forward in a meaningful way are the dreams that connect with something deep inside you, that express the way you choose to feel about life.

When your dream is authentic in this way, it has enormous power. It is your own source of continuing energy, a perpetual energy machine driving your efforts. When your life is running low on energy, an authentic dream is something you can return to at any time to replenish that energy.

What does such an authentic dream feel like? You've got a long day ahead, a lot of work to do, so you plan to get an early start. The alarm goes off at 4:30 a.m. You didn't get to bed until 11:45 the night before, and you don't feel like getting up. Even so, an authentic dream will get you up. That's what it feels like.

You've made fifteen phone calls and received no for an answer fifteen times. You pick up the phone and dial the sixteenth call, and then the seventeenth and eighteenth and twentieth and the fiftieth if necessary. Because you have a dream that won't let you do anything else. That's what it feels like. It feels like power, because it is. It is the power you've had all along, and when you activate it and focus it in a truly meaningful direction, great value is created.

That's your starting point for accessing the amazing worldwide achievement machine—a dream that is authentic and compelling for you. And by the way, your dream can be anything. It doesn't have to be reasonable. It doesn't have to practical. It doesn't have to be something that's intended to save the world. It can be completely self-serving. Because even if it is, even if you can't imagine how your dream will be of any value to anyone else, it will be. When you plug your dream into the worldwide achievement machine, it will benefit many, many other people. We'll look at how that all works a little later on. For now, know that it will. Your dream will be of great benefit to many more people than just you, no matter what it is. What's important is that it's something truly meaningful to you.

So, don't put any limits on it. Don't feel guilty about it. Don't feel embarrassed about it. Feel proud of it. Feel proud within yourself about it. Feel completely ok with that dream, as long as it is really, truly yours. The important thing is for your dream to be something that really gets you going and keeps you going. Feed it into the amazing worldwide achievement machine, and real, lasting value comes out.

Beyond your dream being completely authentic and meaningful, there are other factors necessary to create value using the amazing worldwide achievement machine. One important factor is responsibility. You've got to be willing to take full responsibility for your own life. The machine doesn't give you any credit for flimsy excuses, or even not-so-flimsy excuses, or for blaming your troubles on someone else. To the amazing worldwide achievement machine, excuses mean exactly nothing. The machine doesn't care whose fault it is that you didn't get something done, or whose fault it is that things are the way they are. What matters is that you're willing to step up and take responsibility for your own dream and for the achievement of that dream and for getting through the obstacles and challenges that you must get through in order to achieve that dream. What matters is that you acknowledge and accept complete responsibility for creating the value necessary to achieve your dream.

Keep in mind that the amazing worldwide achievement machine doesn't create value out of nothing. Rather, it takes value that is already within you and it transforms that value into things other people can use, and into things that you too can use and enjoy. The value is already within you somewhere, though not yet fully expressed or manifested. The value exists as your thoughts, your skills, your commitments, and yes, your dreams. The process of achievement is the process of connecting with your own abundant inner value and manifesting it into specific instances of outer value and expression. It is that process for which you must take full and loving responsibility.

A big part of taking responsibility is taking action. The reason the amazing worldwide achievement machine represents such a powerful opportunity is because it harnesses and focuses and directs the power of people doing what they do best. The way for you to participate in that opportunity is by doing whatever it is you do best. And that involves taking action.

You can't just sit back and toss your dream into the machine and expect it to come true. No, that's not how it works. You can't just sit in your car in the driver's seat and expect the car to go where you want it to go. You've got to turn the key, you've got to pay attention to the road, put your foot on the accelerator, constantly adjust the steering wheel, put your foot on the brake when you need to, pay attention to the road signs, know where you are, know where you want to go, and perform the actions that are necessary to control the car.

The amazing worldwide achievement machine is the same way. You've got to do the actions that are necessary to take control of the achievement of your own dream, and to guide it, and to maintain that control. You'll have to execute course corrections when things get a little bit off track, as will occasionally happen. Think about the course corrections you make when driving your car. You tell your car where you want it to go by pointing it in the right direction, and you have to stay with it. You can't just point it in the right direction and put it on cruise control and expect it to get there. You have to constantly make corrections along the way. It's the same with achievement. You have to continue taking action to keep your efforts on track.

The great thing is, technology has given you enormous leverage in taking action. We've been looking at the example of driving your car. Your car represents extremely powerful technology for getting you where you want to go. If you didn't have the car, the actions you would take would be similar, but a lot less powerful. They would have a lot less influence. If you didn't have a car and you wanted to go somewhere, you'd have to walk. If you wanted to go a long distance, such as 200 miles, and you were walking, it would take you several days, or even longer. In a car, the journey would be done in just a few hours. Yet whether you walk or drive a car, you still have to take action.

The nature of that action would be different, though, depending on whether you were walking or driving. When walking, your actions are more physically intense. When you're driving, there is still some physical aspect to what you're doing, yet the effort is much more mentally intense. For example, you have to pay attention to how fast you're going, pay attention to the other cars on the road, keep track of how much gas is in your gas tank, and numerous other things like that. Those things are all very important, and they're all primarily mental exercises. Generally, the more your actions are leveraged by technology, the more powerful they are, but also the more complex they become. It's a lot more complex to drive a car than it is to walk. Yet you've learned to do that. You're capable of doing that. And it gives you great leverage. Piloting an aircraft is even more complex, and even more powerful, because it gets you there even quicker, thus providing increased leverage. It's more powerful to send an email than it is to write a letter and put it in an envelope and mail it, because the email gets there immediately. But you have to learn how to do it. It's more complicated. Once you get it set up and learn how, though, it can be much more powerful. It takes less physical effort but more mental effort.

So, to tap into the value of the amazing worldwide achievement machine you have to take action. And action often means thinking action, particularly when you're leveraging your efforts with powerful technology. Thinking is hard work. That's why so many people are reluctant to do it. It's well worth the trouble, though, because the more thought you put into what you're doing, the more influential and effective it will be.

What else do you need to make use of the amazing worldwide achievement machine? You must have respect and consideration for other people. Because if you treat other people like dirt, the machine is not going to work very well. Others won't want to do things for you. If you expect to get value from someone else without giving equivalent value in return, it's not going to work. The machine will break down. It's like trying to get an air conditioner to work when you unplug it from the wall. If you don't put any energy into it you won't get anything out of it. The amazing worldwide achievement machine works the same way. You've got to first put value in, and then you get value out. What the machine does is transform value. The machine does not create value out of nothing. But it can do a fantastic job of taking raw energy and raw value and transforming it into the precise value you wish to have. It's your job to put that value into it in the first place. You must have respect and consideration for the other parts of the machine, for the machine itself, for the individuals who make up the machine. We're referring to it as a machine, but as I've said before, it's made up of individuals—each person a unique individual, with his or her own desires, own dreams, own reasons for participating in the worldwide achievement machine.

The amazing worldwide achievement machine is ready and waiting for you to take the controls. With a real, authentic dream that means the world to you, you can choose to take responsibility, take action, leverage your actions with clear and focused thoughts, and interact with others in a positive, respectful way. Soon enough, with sufficient action and commitment, your dream will come fully to life.

The Power of Ten Billion Dreams

The Dream Economy

The difference between what we do and what we are capable of doing would suffice to solve most of the world's problems.
— Mohandas K. Gandhi

There's the life you are living right now, and then there's another life, not yet lived though desperately desired, inside of you. Now, right now, this very day, you have the best opportunity anyone has ever had to fully and richly live the life of your dreams. That's not a metaphorical statement or hyperbole. It is a real, practical truth.

Let's take it one step further. Not only do you have the opportunity to fulfill your most treasured, authentic dreams, you could soon find yourself in serious trouble if you don't choose to do so. Yes, it's a spectacular opportunity. And with the way things are going, with the tectonic changes that are taking place in today's world, you may not have any other choice.

Make no mistake about it. The world is a radically different place than it was just a year ago, and the pace of change is accelerating. Most of the old assumptions around when you were growing up and getting a formal education have been dead and buried for years. Even many of the new assumptions are out of date.

We're quickly moving from an economy that was based on stuff to an economy that's based on dreams. Yes, we still have lots of material stuff. But that's not what's driving the world forward. Everybody still eats food, and there are more people than ever eating more varieties of food than ever. Yet how many farmers do you know? Chances are, you don't know any. Hundreds of years ago, almost everybody worked on a farm. Now, it's just a tiny percentage of the population, yet we eat more food than ever. What happened? The production of food became outrageously efficient. That's a good thing. It keeps us fed while freeing us to focus on other things.

In the last few dozen decades, that's precisely what we've

been focusing on—things. More specifically, on inventing and manufacturing and distributing and using all sorts of amazing things. Pay a visit to Walmart, and it's all there for you to see. In historical terms, it is embarrassingly affordable. The average modern-day working-class family has a significantly higher standard of living than European royalty of a couple hundred years ago.

Lately, all that stuff has taken on a new theme—digital information. It is transforming the world of stuff faster than a wildfire. The information that used to be locked up in solid objects can now be instantly transported to any spot on the globe. The music industry and the travel industry were among the first to be radically altered by this dynamic. Almost nobody buys compact discs anymore. Why would they when they can instantly download the information? And nobody goes to a travel agent to pick up an airline ticket. Airline tickets are no longer physical things. They're numbers that can instantly be e-mailed to your smartphone.

Yes, we will always need and use physical stuff, just as we will always need food. But our focus is largely turning away from the stuff and toward the opportunities it gives us to interact with each other. Just as the modernization of agriculture freed us from the need to toil in the fields, the information revolution is quickly enabling more and more people to live richer and more fulfilling lives.

It may not seem that way if you've lost your job to an industrial robot, or if the video rental store you worked at has closed because everyone is now downloading movies instead of renting DVDs. But if you have the courage to step back and view the situation from an objective perspective, what you'll see is opportunity. Admittedly, it is a very challenging opportunity, but then that's the best kind. If your job has been replaced by a computer or a high-speed internet connection, what's your best strategy going forward? Is it a good idea to look for another job that will soon be in danger of being outsourced or automated? Of course not. You've already been burned by that. No, your best prospect for creating value is to do something that no machine can do. But then there's the prospect of your job being outsourced to a low-wage country. That being the case, it's necessary to take your strategy one step further. So in addition to doing something that no machine can replicate, you want to be doing something that no other person can replicate.

What in the world would that be? What is it that you can do, that no one else can do? Here's what. You are the only person ever in the history of the world who can be you. You are the only person who can achieve the fulfillment of your own unique, authentic dreams. As we've seen, the opportunity for doing that is here and now. And in this quickly changing world, the necessity is also here.

If you ignore your dreams, you could very well be ignoring your most valuable asset. What if you were living on the street, eating out of garbage bins, begging for food, and yet you had a $20 million stock portfolio that you never touched? Does that sound crazy? It could be even more foolish to be struggling through the day-to-day details of life without paying attention the the dreams living inside you.

In fact, in our aggressively interconnected world, your greatest opportunity is to be you. Your dreams are what enable you to do that. Are you a generous person? The greatest gift you can give is to be authentically you. In living your dreams you give that unique and valuable gift of yourself, your beautiful and authentic self, to all of life.

Think about the implications of an economy that's focused not on material things, but on individual dreams. Although the massive industrialization of work and life has raised our standard of living, it has also tended to make our interactions with each other more transactional. The industrialization of the last couple of hundred years has standardized the products and services we consume. You can purchase the same turkey sandwich from Subway in Austin, Aruba, Adelaide or Amsterdam. Along with that, unfortunately, has come a standardization of our interactions. We're all too often treated as just another transaction instead of as a unique individual. A world based on dreams changes all that.

Technology has advanced to the point where high volume, efficient production does not necessarily mean mass, cookie-cutter production. The bad news is that robots have replaced auto workers. The good news is that the automobile you purchase can be customized to your exact specifications, without a lot of extra cost or delay. There are more than 1,300 ways you can combine the various options when ordering a Volkswagen Tiguan from the digitized factory that produces it.

What all this means is that we no longer have to treat each other as numbers. Innovative providers of products and services are quickly jumping on the new opportunities to deliver unique, individualized experiences to their customers. The technology is able to provide you with precisely what you desire. In such an environment, the onus is on you to know and to seek and to fulfill precisely what you do desire.

How do you go from living in a material world, that's obsessed with material things, to living in a world that's driven forward by dreams? We'll look into this in much greater detail later, but here's a powerful question you can ask yourself right now that will point the way. You probably already have a lot of great stuff, and there's more cool stuff that you'd like to have. Take all of it into consideration, and then ask yourself this. What wonderful, outstanding, fascinating and fulfilling things can I do with all this stuff?

Stop looking at your material possessions as mere objects that you own mainly to impress your friends. Start thinking of them as powerful tools, because many of them are. Realize that you have all these great tools, and figure out what you would do if you could do absolutely anything you wanted to do. The chances are very good that somewhere in there, you'll find a way. It won't be easy, but then easy is overrated. You've had enough easy. Now is your opportunity for rich, and joyful, truly satisfying and fulfilling. What exactly can you do with your time and your tools and your other resources, your knowledge, experience and passion, that will bring a truly outstanding level of fulfillment to your life?

You already know the answer. Somewhere inside, you know. The hard part is letting yourself see it. It's emotionally difficult and at the same time spiritually liberating.

We're moving toward a world in which individual dreams are enabled and encouraged. It's a world where the dreams of one person can resonate with the dreams of others and combine with those other dreams, bouncing off each other, strengthening each other and building on each other. Our increasing interconnectedness enables us to transition from a stuff-based economy into a dream-based economy. Sure, we'll still have stuff—plenty of it. It's necessary. It's useful. But increasingly, we don't have stuff for the sake of stuff. We have material possessions and achievements for the sake of living dreams. More and more people are realizing that the ultimate goal in life is not to accumulate a lot of stuff, but to accumulate a lot of meaning and fulfillment. It doesn't mean there's anything wrong with having a lot of stuff. It means we're learning to put that stuff in perspective.

Love people, not things; use things, not people.
— Spencer W. Kimball

That's exactly what we're now in a position to do, with positive purpose and effectiveness. We must love people and the dreams that people have, and then make use of the all material things we have—the vehicles, the structures and buildings and systems and products and networks—make use of those things, but always with an eye toward fulfilling and expressing dreams, the beautiful, unique individual dreams of each person. Those dreams are not bogus, mass-produced dreams, not cheap dreams that have no meaning, but real, substantial dreams. We have the opportunity to encourage other people to dream, and live our own dreams in such a way that encourages and brings out and resonates and connects to the dreams in other people. That's how life is lived in a dream-based economy. It's an economy where every person has the potential for great fulfillment.

Yes, there are massive challenges, but the opportunities are even more compelling. This is a time of great change and tumult, because a large swath of assumptions have been plowed under. What remains is a fertile field where dreams can take root and flourish, provided they are carefully chosen and diligently nurtured.

It's not easy to dream. This is not some easy walk in the park. It's difficult to live your dreams. In fact, it's more difficult to live your dreams than it is to go and get a job where you do the same thing every day and you get paid just enough money to survive but you really don't have a life. No, it's much harder to live your dreams than that.

It takes initiative. You've got to dig into yourself. You think that's easy? It's not. It hurts. It can be painful. It can take an enormous amount of effort. It can be a lot of trouble and inconvenience. It can be embarrassing. But it's also fulfilling and enriching, not only for your own life but for the lives of those around you. And by doing the difficult work of living your dreams, you avoid the unbearable regret that would come from a life not fully lived.

It's difficult, but definitely worth the trouble. It's worth all the effort, the pain, the inconvenience, and the embarrassment. It's worth the time. It's worth the commitment, the persistence, and whatever it takes to live your dream. Because that's where your unique value is. That's where you'll find fulfillment and richness.

Would you prefer to sit back and let somebody else do all the work? Sorry, but that's just an impossible fantasy. You're not here just so somebody else can take care of you. You're here to live your own life, to fulfill your own unique dreams.

You owe it to life to dream. You owe it to yourself to dream. Within you is a beautiful dream. You owe it to life to live that dream, not to hide from it, not to run from it, not to cower in the corner and hope somebody takes care of you. But to get out there, to get your face in the wind, get cold, get wet, get sore, get exhausted. It sounds like a lot of needless trouble but once you do it, it feels good. Get busy. Make some mistakes. Do things. Get stuff done. Take some chances. Take some risks. Get out there and live your dream. Because that's who you are.

Right now, you're living in a world where the accumulation of thousands of years of progress gives you the unprecedented opportunity, and the obligation, to live the life of your dreams. Grab that opportunity, fulfill that obligation, and experience the rich, fulfilling life that is your destiny.

New Paradigm of Dreams

Yesterday is but today's memory, and tomorrow is today's dream.

— Khalil Gibran

If you've attended school in the last 50 years, you've most likely been educated for a world that no longer exists. You've been taught to get along, to follow directions, and to do so in a skillful, efficient way. But the problem is, there are no longer any good jobs like that. No one is going to pay you much, if anything at all, to do that kind of work. Why? Because we've created powerful, adaptable machines and automated systems that do a vast amount of routine, repetitive, unimaginative work. We've created amazingly powerful machines that follow certain instructions much faster and more reliably than any person could ever hope to do. If your idea of creating value is following directions without having to put any of your own creativity and judgment into the work, you've been replaced by a machine, or soon will be. Though that may seem like bad news, when you step back and look at the big picture of your possibilities, it is actually very good news. But it definitely takes some getting used to.

The world of your parents and grandparents was a world of hierarchies. But most of the hierarchies have now been flattened. And the implication of that is, when the hierarchy is flattened, you are on top. You're the boss. You're the manager. You're the CEO of your own work. And you're also the bottom. You're the worker.

You may be employed by someone else, but in a flattened hierarchy, you're more of a peer than a subordinate or a boss, no matter what your title. That has enormous implications. It has all sorts of positive valuable possibilities, but it also has many pitfalls. If you continue to think the way you've been taught to think, that you live in a hierarchical world, a world where there are many levels of workers above you and below you, that's really no longer the case.

It presents incredible possibilities, but they're different possibilities. They're different opportunities. They're not the same as before.

It's a revolutionary time. The world is undergoing massive changes. And eventually those changes will mean that more people than ever before will live better lives than ever before. It's certainly happened in the past.

Think about a couple of hundred years ago, how daily life was for most people. Three or four hundred years ago, the majority of people lived in rural areas and worked the land. Much of the food they ate was food they grew in their gardens or on their farms, or it was food their neighbors grew. The way they got around was walking. Their means of communication was talking to people in person or occasionally sending a letter, or sending word with a traveler. They had no cell phones, they had no television, they had no radio, they had no internet, they had no iPods. Their form of entertainment was whatever they could come up with on their own. Of course they didn't really have the luxury of having much time for entertainment. Sometimes they played games. Not video games, not online massively multiplayer games, but simple card games or board games or sports. Their entertainment was walking through the woods. On very special occasions they would be entertained by other people, maybe by people singing or telling jokes or playing instruments or acting in a play. Only the very fortunate got to have much of that kind of entertainment.

Such a life was good for some people, but it was unimaginably hard by our standards. Yet people survived. It was all they knew. It was the best that they knew. And they might could hope to marry nobility or royalty, but it was a one in a million chance. Otherwise they didn't have much hope of advancing themselves. They pretty much remained in whatever station in life they were born to. Occasionally there were people who were very ambitious and rose out of their mediocrity, but it didn't happen very much. By our standards today, people back then lived simple lives. Some of them could read and write, but many couldn't. Those who could read had the luxury of reading books, when they could get them. That's how they lived.

Then the industrial revolution came along. And it was a huge shock. We're still feeling the effects of that shock. Some cultures still have not fully adjusted to it. It was traumatic. And yet, look what it did for people. Look how significantly it raised the standard of living for people all over the world. Not only did it raise the standard of living for people rich and poor, but it gave many, many more people the opportunity to take control of their own lives and to raise their positions in life.

Had you been living during this time you would have felt the revolutionary aspect of it. Instead of being stuck in the same job your father had, and your grandfather had, and your great-grandfather had, you would have had more options. You could have chosen to learn a highly complex technical skill, so as to advance yourself. You could have become a merchant and been an initial participant in the free market economy that has now been booming (relatively speaking) for the past 300 years. The free market based economy has produced levels of wealth that would have been completely unimaginable a few hundred years ago. In just a short period it has spread that wealth far and wide. It has raised standards of living not just for the rich but for everyone. In countries such as the United States, even the poor are extremely wealthy by historical standards.

So the industrial revolution not only made the whole world wealthier, it also gave individuals the opportunity to advance themselves, to take control of their own destinies. And now, all that is making a quantum jump to a much higher level.

Think of what would happen if somebody from several hundred years ago were suddenly to be dropped into our modern society. Let's imagine he's a man who is about thirty years old, who had grown up and spent his life living off the land, living in a simple society where to get around you had to walk, to communicate you had to talk in person, for entertainment you read a book, and if you had to go long distances you would have to get on a ship to cross the sea or join a caravan to cross great distances on land. Imagine someone from that time, who is adjusted to that life, suddenly having to deal with the complexities of our modern world, suddenly needing to know a whole new set of skills in order to get by on a day to day basis.

Let's say this person lives in the suburbs of a large city and works at a job five miles away. He has to drive a car to get there every day. So first of all, he has to learn how to drive. Even before he can do that, though, he has to learn what a car is. The whole concept of driving an automobile is foreign to him. Think about that. You probably grew up with your parents carrying you from place to place in a motor vehicle. Although riding in that vehicle did not teach you all the skills needed for driving, it did teach you at a very early age the concepts behind driving a car. Even as a child you were able to understand the need to follow where the road leads, to stop at traffic lights and stop signs, to avoid with other cars, and to know the name of the streets where important places, such as your house, the grocery store and your school were located. So you are familiar with the concept and many of the implications of being transported on a daily basis in a motor vehicle. As a result, even before you started driving you knew about parking the car, starting the engine, locking the doors, and turning on the headlights at night. A person from hundreds of years ago would first have to become familiar with the very concept of driving, and then on top of that would have to learn how to drive, and then on top of that would have to learn his way around, learn the names of the roads, the rules, how to start the car, learn how to buy gasoline and maintain the car by changing the oil and making sure the tires have the correct pressure. Then of course the person would have to buy the car and would have to negotiate a car loan and make payments, and have a bank account with which to do that. Just about all of that would be completely foreign to a person of several hundred years ago.

When our person from the past arrived at work, he would have to know how to use a computer, how to use the telephone, and voice mail. He would need to learn the concept of email and the concept of going to a web page. Even someone from as recent as 20 years ago, if that person were to see a modern-day a commercial on TV that included a web address, would have no idea what it was. If the commercial said "go

The Power of Ten Billion Dreams

to www.myproduct.com" the person from 20 years ago would have no idea how to do that, how to "go" to the www place. That person might have assumed that "www" was some kind of shopping mall.

In short, a person from several hundred years ago would be totally lost when it comes to the complexities of life in our present-day world. He would have to learn a whole new set of skills. However, he would most certainly be able to do so. With enough motivation, training, persistence and commitment he could do it. In fact, he could probably do it fairly quickly. People are amazingly adaptable.

Indeed, our person from the past could learn how to get around. Instead of going out into the garden to get fresh vegetables, he would soon learn how to go to the supermarket or to restaurants to get food. Instead of gathering firewood and building a fire to cook, he would learn how to use a microwave oven or electric oven or gas grill. Instead of keeping food fresh in a cool stream or a root cellar, he would learn to keep things in the refrigerator. He would have to learn about the unique dangers of living in modern society, such as electricity, and how not to stick his finger in the socket, or not to use a hair dryer in the bathtub. He would need to learn how to open a garage door with a garage door opener (and how to stay out of the way when it closes), how to arm and disarm the intrusion alarm system, how to use a credit card, how to write a check. He would have to become proficient at ordering in a restaurant, going through airport security and getting on an airplane. Someone from several hundred years ago would have no idea how to do any of those things. And yet, that person could most certainly figure it out. Billions of people already have figured all those things out.

Imagine going back four hundred years and telling a group of elite, educated scholars of the time that soon everyone in society would have to learn how to do all the complicated things listed above and more. They surely would have considered it impossible. They would concluded that most "ordinary" people would not be capable of doing those complex things. They would have argued that most people would have to lead simple lives, living in the country, living off the land, living on their farms, picking vegetables from fields and cooking them over an open fire. That's the only life they would know, the "experts" from hundreds of years ago would have argued, and it would not be possible for simple, common people to learn so very many new skills.

But of course, they would have been wrong. Ordinary, everyday people have learned to get along just fine with all the complexities of modern life. More people are learning to do so all the time. Look at countries such as India and China that are becoming industrialized even now at an explosive rate. In those places, people are going from a simple, rural lifestyle to a complex, urban lifestyle, adopting all the latest technologies quickly and intelligently, and making valuable use of all the conveniences of modern life. They're taking to it rapidly. People are flocking into the cities. People who have never driven before are buying automobiles by the millions. People are buying digital televisions, computers, cell phones, and using them with all their complex features. There are more than five billion cell phones in use around the world. In some countries such as Brazil, there are more cell phones than there are people! Something that no one used 25 years ago is now being used by virtually everyone. And they're not just cell phones. They're smart phones. They can get on the Internet, they can send email, and they can browse web pages. They can connect to online social networks. And speaking of social networking, look at how quickly that has spread. Everybody who participates in social networking has learned how to do it just in the last five years or so. People are adaptable. People can learn to do new things very quickly when they're motivated to do so.

And that's the challenge we face now. That's the challenge you face, along with the incredible opportunity of living your dreams. It's a challenge you definitely want to get out in front of. Because it's a challenge that will enable you to magnificently raise your standard of living, higher and higher and higher. We're all moving quickly into a new world. We're emerging from a world shaped by the industrial revolution, where there were hierarchies, where people had to learn to work in factories and had to learn to work for a boss who had a boss who had a boss who had a boss. People had to learn to manage people under them, and manage people who were under the people who were under them. People had to learn to fit into the hierarchy and to do their job as they were told, to produce things, to produce wealth, to produce value. And that's great, because it has brought us a long, long way. It has brought us incredible living standards by historical perspectives. It has brought us incredible lifestyles and options. But the thing is, that era is coming to an end. That era is ending with the flattening of the world. The world is being flattened by advances in information technology. Such a world has profound implications for you, and for your dreams.

The hierarchies that developed during the industrial age were put in place to facilitate communication, division of labor, and specialization. There would be people working in factories who would sit and put one bolt in place all day long, on unit after unit after unit as they passed by on the assembly line. At one time that was the state of art in efficiency. It was Henry Ford's idea, and it was a real breakthrough for its time. Parts were standardized, and the labor was standardized—standardized and specialized and managed through the hierarchy of the organization. People could make good money doing what they were told, doing it tediously all day long, without the need to think or create or question or analyze.

But now that has all been replaced. All that tedious work has been automated. Human workers are not needed to do that anymore. We have powerful, flexible machines to take care of it. The shift is even more profound in occupations that deal with information. People used to sit around and do calculations all day long. People used to file information and retrieve information all day long. All that was replaced long ago by computers. No one is needed to do that kind of work. Furthermore, the hierarchies and levels of management are no longer needed. People can access information directly, and they can access each other directly.

So we have to figure out a new way for this to work. We have the capability to create much more value than ever before. But we're able to do it without nearly as many people. In the United States, we are manufacturing more things than we've ever manufactured, but are using a whole lot fewer people to do so. The same thing happened a century and a half ago in agriculture when it became mechanized. Food production grew, but the number of people working in agriculture plummeted.

We are able to do more, in terms of making stuff and ware-housing it and delivering it and keeping track of it, with fewer people. That's an opportunity and a problem. It's a problem because it puts people out of a job. But it's an opportunity too because it frees those people to do more creative things. And on a personal level, that is the opportunity as well as the challenge—to be unique and creative.

So where does that come from? What enables you to be unique and creative? Your dream. Your ability to dream. That's why dreams are so vitally important now. They've always been important. But now, more so than ever, they're essential. You must know who you are deep inside. You've got to know what your purpose is and you've got to express that purpose. That is how you create value in the world today.

Being a dreamer used to be an option. In fact, it used to carry a certain stigma. After all, people were needed to man the factory assembly lines and to work as filing clerks. There was no time for dreaming. There was work to be done. Now we have great and wonderful machines to do all our physical, tedious work. It's time to revive those dreams.

Let's say you lived in a house that didn't have an automatic dishwasher. After each meal, the dishes would need to be washed by hand. Then, suddenly, a dishwasher is installed in your kitchen. Instead of washing the dishes, you have to figure out something else to do with your time. It's great to have the dishwasher. It's an opportunity, but it's also a challenge. Washing the dishes enabled you to create value, to make a contribution. Now, you can still get the dishes cleaned, but you have the challenge of finding something meaningful to do with that extra time. That is precisely the situation the whole world finds itself in right now. Just as our time traveler from hundreds of years ago learned how to use email, each of us is fully capable of adapting and thriving in a world that depends on dreams.

In many ways, we're coming full circle. Because hundreds

of years ago, before the world was industrialized, people had to be more self sufficient than they are now. Then came the industrial age, and people could specialize in one particular area to create a lot of value by doing one thing and not much else. Those days have come to an end. Today, we have both the opportunity and the challenge of becoming significantly more well-rounded. Life is no longer about sitting on an assembly line and screwing a certain size nut onto a certain size bolt all day long. People from all walks of life have the opportunity to live richly and abundantly, to live lives that are continually fascinating, doing work that is appropriate to who they are and in line with their passions and with what interests them.

But along with that opportunity comes the responsibility to do it. We have to learn how to dream. We have to connect with who we are. It's an individual responsibility, because dreams can't be mass produced. That's not what dreams are. Dreams come from within you. Sure, there are certain universal values that we all ascribe to, and those are closely connected to our dreams. Yet the power of a dream comes from within you. It comes from your own individual purpose, from your perspective, from the way you look out and see the world.

As we plunge headlong into a massively interconnected civilization, countless problems arise because things are changing so quickly. Those problems are serious and widespread. But the thing is, they're problems of success. We've created a world that is enormously productive. We can spit out billions of things—manufactured products, software products, entertainment products, information products, books, CDs, cars, TVs, communication networks, yachts, airplanes, buildings, houses. We can produce all sorts of great things. We have the capability. It all exists. We have the resources, the materials, the knowledge. We can make a lot of stuff. We know how to do that. We've become enormously successful at it. In fact, some would say we've become too successful at it, that we focus much too much on things because we're so good at making them and distributing them. Now the challenge is to turn that focus inward and to make that stuff meaningful. Now the challenge is to use all that stuff to truly enrich our lives, to use the amazing worldwide achievement machine to bring real richness to life. That's our opportunity and that's our challenge.

There's no single answer to the challenges and problems we face. But there is a place where we can each find our own answer, each of us individually. There's a place where you can find that answer. There's a place where your neighbor can find that answer. There's a place where I can find that answer. And that is, in our dreams, the dreams that come from our purpose, the dreams that are authentic. The desires we have. We have them for a reason.

Have you ever thought about that? You have your desires for a reason. They're not there to annoy you. They're not there to tease you. They're not there to make you regretful. They are there to push you forward in a direction you're perfectly suited to go. They're there to motivate you, to inspire you to do what you do best, to live life from your very own perspective and to give to life the special value that you have to give. That's what your dreams are for. That's why they're there. They are not there to cause you pain. They are there to cause you joy and to enable you to give joy to many, many others. Yes, that's what your dreams are for. And that is where you'll find the most meaningful answers, by looking within yourself, by feeling those positive feelings you feel when you connect with your dreams. What is the most effective way to spend your life? Understand your purpose. Understand your dreams. What you really wish to do is what you're best suited to do.

Your purpose. Some people (myself included) believe it comes from God. Others see it as coming from random chance. But regardless of where it comes from, it is unquestionably there. Whether you believe that you were created for a certain purpose or whether you believe that you just got that way at random, the fact is that you do indeed have a purpose. You can feel it. You are here, regardless of how you got here. And you have a special set of qualities. You have a special set of passions. You have a special set of interests, and things that you're good at. And you are particularly good at doing the things that you enjoy. That's what you do best. You know that. If you're doing something you love to do, you can feel yourself putting yourself into it one hundred percent. When you're doing what you love, you give all you have, and reach deep down inside yourself to find the persistence, the commitment, the excellence and the effectiveness to get it done.

So don't you think you should be doing what means the most to you? Don't you think you should be finding what that special something is, and connecting to it and working out a way to express it, to express who you are, to express the best that you can be?

That's where your dreams come in. That's why you owe it to life to dream. That's why you owe it to life to do what you love to do. You owe it to yourself. You owe it to the people around you. You owe it to your family. It's your obligation. You're here. You're breathing life's air. You're eating life's food. You're taking up space. You owe it to all of life to make a contribution. I owe it to life. We all owe it to each other to be the absolute best we can be and to express our own unique purpose, because that's what we came with when we arrived. That's what we developed through years of life. We've honed that purpose and we've made it more rich. What you owe to life, and the best you'll find in life, is to follow your purpose, to live your dream.

The Power of Ten Billion Dreams

Dreams Change the World

So many nights I sit and dream of the ocean.
God I wish I was sailing again.

— Jimmy Buffett

I have a dream of taking my own sailboat all the way from Corpus Christi to Barbados. But why haven't I already done it? If it means so much to me, why did I wait until just recently to start preparing for that journey?

I could come up with plenty of great-sounding, perfectly reasonable excuses. But the real reason is that, until recently, I just assumed such a thing was a frivolous undertaking. To my mind, I had many more important things to do.

Indeed, it is frivolous. I don't need to sail to Barbados, or anywhere else for that matter. I merely want to. Yes, I feel very much at home, very much in my element when I'm out on the water at the helm of a boat. It's a visceral feeling that can't adequately be put into words. It resonates powerfully with something deep inside me. As I write these words, at just the thought of being out on the ocean I can feel a positive change come over me. I can sense a longing and a desire to be sailing because I know how right it feels.

Even so, what right do I have to go off sailing in the warm, clear waters of the Caribbean when there are people starving in this world? By what measure do I feel entitled to sit at anchor sipping a perfectly chilled glass of viognier and watching a magnificent sunset, when so many people have lost their homes due to foreclosure? It seems almost heartless of me to be enjoying my life when there are so many people struggling.

It's a question as old as humanity. What is the purpose of life? What are we here for? I have always had a strong sense that we're here to help others. That sense has guided me in writing more than 5,000 Daily Motivator messages. With each message, I seek to write something that will genuinely be of help to those who read it.

But there's a followup question to the answer that we're here to help others. If we are indeed here to help others, then what are others here for? Though at first blush that question may seem like nothing more than a clever twist of words and logic, there's actually some powerful insight in it. To say we're here to help others sounds very nice and altruistic, but it also avoids the substance of the question. After all, what exactly are we here to help others do?

In assuming that my dream of sailing across the ocean was not worth following because of its frivolity, I was doing pretty much the same thing. I was sidestepping the big important question about the meaning of life. In my zeal to be of service to others, I was pushing that question off on them, and making other people responsible for my own sense of purpose.

So what does all this navel gazing have to do with the power of dreams?

Dreams—even frivolous ones—have the power to change the world. A dream that is authentic and unfettered carries with it more than enough energy for the fulfillment of that dream. But here's the problem. If you don't really, truly feel worthy of living your dream, it won't be authentic, and it will be severely limited. It won't have any energy. It won't be of any value to you. It won't be of any value to anyone.

So what exactly was making me feel unworthy and suppressing my dream? I was making a common, yet flawed assumption. I sincerely wanted to be of service to others, which is great. However, I assumed that the quickest, most powerful and effective way to do that was to deny my own personal desires and dreams. That's where I was seriously mistaken.

Yes, when you wish to help others you can make some progress by ignoring your own desires and focusing all your energy on others. Eventually, though, that energy runs out. By denying yourself, you soon have nothing left to give to others. I spent years making several attempts at writing another book, but something was missing. My intention was to publish a book that would encourage readers to live their dreams, but

The Power of Ten Billion Dreams

it wasn't working. Something was simply not there. What was missing, it turned out, was my very own dream.

To encourage others to live their dreams while at the same time ignoring my own dreams is the height of hypocrisy. It's really pretty arrogant, too, not to mention condescending.

If the reason we're here is to help others, what are others here for? That question just dances around the real question which of course is this: what is the purpose of life? Focusing on my own dream has led me to answer that question in a way that feels right. The answer I've found is definitely not politically correct, but it has the clear ring of truth to it. On the surface it seems quite selfish, yet when you stand back and look at the big picture, it is not selfish at all.

To understand what my answer is, ask yourself this. What are you good at doing? What things are you most effective at accomplishing? You are undoubtedly the most highly effective when you're doing what you enjoy. How well do you perform when you're doing something you absolutely detest? Well, you might be able to turn in an acceptable performance, but you also know without a doubt that it's not anywhere near the best you could do. Ah, but when you're doing what you truly love to do, you're great at it.

When you love to do something, whether it's singing, playing golf, creating web pages, or growing gardenias, you'll do it every time you get the chance. All that practice makes you great. All that passion makes you even better. Put the practice and the passion together, and you're putting in a top notch performance.

Why do you have an appetite for food? Because you require food for survival. Why do you get thirsty? Because you must have water in order to stay alive. These things are just common sense, right?

So, why do you have the capability to experience joy? Is it just some vestigial function that really serves no purpose in your life? Of course not. You are able to experience joy for a very good reason. In a state of joy, you operate at your highest level of effectiveness. That puts joy right up there with eating, breathing and drinking water as an essential element of your life.

What are we here for? What is the purpose of life? The purpose of life is to enjoy its richness and wonder.

That's it. That's the answer I've settled on. I know, I know, it sounds terribly trivial and self-serving. Here's the thing, though. When you're truly enjoying life, you're giving your absolute best to it. When you're enjoying life, you're fully utilizing your unique skills, calling upon your wealth of wisdom and experience, and creating new value. What could possibly be more helpful to others, than that?

Look at it this way. If you were sick, hungry, broke and homeless, and had exhausted all your options, who would you rather turn to for help—someone who is miserable, with no joy in his life, or someone who is happy and fulfilled, and who is enjoying life to the fullest? I can only answer for myself, but I know I would choose the happy, fulfilled person to lift me up. I have a feeling you would, too. The undeniable fact is, people who are enjoying their lives can be vastly more helpful to you than people who are miserable.

Think of all the magnificent beauty in this world, and in the universe. If you were not here to appreciate and enjoy it, what would be the point of it? If no one was around to find joy in the magnificence of creation, why would it even be there? Joy feels wonderful for a reason. It feels right for a reason. The reason is because it is not only your good fortune and privilege to feel joy, it is your fundamental responsibility.

Imagine that you're an artist, and you have created a stunningly beautiful painting, and it's hanging in a gallery for all to see, but no one ever notices it. How would you feel about that? Would you be inclined to paint another? The next time you have the opportunity to watch a magnificent sunset, think about that, and take the time to watch. And to enjoy.

All of this doesn't mean that life is meant to always be enjoyable. We know from experience that it can often be very difficult and painful. Those painful times have their place and they have their value. But they're not what we aspire to. Nobody fondly dreams of living in pain or dismay. In fact, it is usually the prospect of getting beyond the pain that gives us the energy to indeed work our way through those painful and difficult times. And by the same measure, it is by living through the difficult times that we develop a deeper appreciation for the value of the good, enjoyable experiences in life.

If the ultimate purpose of life is indeed to enjoy its richness and wonder, if it is in fact your responsibility to fill your life with as much joy and fulfillment as possible, then dreams provide an ideal mechanism for fulfilling that purpose. Dreams give you a specific direction in which to focus your attention, your efforts and your energy.

Are you worthy of living your dreams? That's really not the issue. Yes, of course you're worthy of living the most joyful and magnificent life you can imagine. But the thing is, it's not a question of whether you're worthy. It is your obligation to live your most authentic dreams. It's your obligation to the miraculous existence that you have the incredible good fortune to experience.

Your joy and fulfillment create possibilities for even more joy and fulfillment. The value you create gives birth to opportunities for many others to create and enjoy value. There is not a fixed, limited amount of value in life. There is not a fixed, limited supply of fulfillment. In fact, the more fulfillment you have in your own life, the more opportunities it creates for many other people to be fulfilled.

I know firsthand how powerful just a single dream can be. I've seen it in my own life and in the lives of those around me. That's why I seek to encourage as many people as possible to follow their authentic dreams. And even though I cannot grasp even a fraction of the magnificent possibilities, I know that the combined power of billions of individual dreams can change the whole world for the better in many wonderful and profound ways.

You know that too, if you'll just stop and feel it. Think of something you truly wish to experience in your life, not because it would impress other people, not because it is something that everybody else has, but because it is something that resonates with the very essence of who you are. Go ahead right now and dream. It doesn't matter if your dream is practical or reasonable. What matters is that it's something fundamentally meaningful to you. Pull that dream to the front of your awareness and completely focus on it. Imagine living your life when that dream has been fully realized. Feel the power, the joy, and the sense of satisfaction and fulfillment.

Imagine how the world will look to you when that most treasured dream of yours is completely fulfilled. Imagine how your daily life will be in such a world. In your mind, see, hear, taste and touch all the details. Now feel the power of your authentic desire to live that dream. It's a compelling force. When you fill your awareness with it, you have the courage to stand up to any challenge, as well as the energy and resourcefulness to work through every problem. Following your dreams will dramatically improve your own life, but it doesn't stop there. In the process of following your dreams, you cannot help but support and enable the dreams of many, many others.

The amazing thing is, this happens without any kind of centralized planning or grand organized scheme. It is completely natural for the dreams of one person to inspire and enable the dreams of others.

Somewhere in central Florida, a young woman dreams of becoming a minister. She applies for admittance to a theological seminary and is accepted. She gets a modest scholarship, but needs additional money to pay the rest of the tuition as well as her living expenses. As it happens, this young woman finds a part-time job working at a boat building company. The company builds sailing yachts. Why is there a market for sailing yachts? What enables the company to stay in business and to provide this young ministry student with a place to earn money? Because somewhere, someone dreams of sailing across the ocean to an island like Barbados.

In Providenciales, in the Turks and Caicos islands, a middle aged man has just moved back home to the island where he was born, after working for more than twenty-five years as a cook in some of Boston's finest restaurants. He dreams of owning a small restaurant on the island, a place where he can continue to indulge his passion for gourmet cooking while also enjoying the island life that is his heritage. With the money he has saved from years of hard work, he leases a space on Coconut Road, near the Turtle Cove Marina, and opens for business. Where will his customers come from? Some of them will be sailors passing through, on their way from the US mainland to destinations such as Grenada, Antigua and Barbados.

Somewhere else in the world, someone is reading a book about dreams. As she reads about the dreams of others, she feels a stirring deep within her own unique purpose. Suddenly, it's clear to her what she must do. A dream to build a school for children in Africa begins to take shape. Somewhere else, someone reading the same book dreams of hiking the full length of the Appalachian Trail, and another person dreams of writing a new iPhone app. In ways that are impossible to know in advance, in ways that could never be anticipated or controlled or planned by even the most well-funded government agency or the most profitable corporation, dreams come to life. In a never-ending upward spiral, those dreams grow, nourished by the value of other dreams, spawning even more dreams in their wake.

Real, authentic dreams are highly contagious. One person's dream draws power from the dreams of others, and then goes on to inspire dreams in yet others. The amazing progress we've experienced since people started walking around this planet has not come from grandiose, utopian, top-down schemes concocted by elite intellectuals. Our progress has come from the power of individual dreams. Our progress has come from people who have acted in their own self-interest, to further their own authentic dreams. We have had the good fortune of discovering along the way that working in cooperation with each other is vastly more effective in furthering self-interest than fighting and abusing each other. We've created a vast, interconnected civilization that enables dreams to feed off each other in unique and creative ways. And though we benefit tremendously from working with each other, it is self-interest—not egotistical self-interest but authentic self-interest, the internal driving desire of dreams, flowing from each person's most fundamental purpose—that moves the world onward and upward.

The Power of Ten Billion Dreams

Life Is Not Fair

You cannot strengthen the weak by weakening the strong. You cannot help small men by tearing down big men. You cannot help the poor by destroying the rich. You cannot lift the wage earner by pulling down the wage payer. You cannot keep out of trouble by spending more than your income. You cannot further the brotherhood of man by inciting class hatreds. You cannot establish security on borrowed money. You cannot build character and courage by taking away a man's initiative and independence. You cannot help men permanently by doing for them what they could and should do for themselves.
— William J. H. Boetcker

Life is not fair. It never has been, and it never will be. Some people are born with powerful advantages. Others are born with crippling disadvantages. For everyone, in different ways and at different times for each person, life is challenging. And although life is not fair, it is dynamic and responsive. Though life is not fair, and though life presents you with endless challenges, you have the opportunity to do something about those challenges. One very important thing you can do is to dream, and use the power of those dreams to triumph even in the face of all the unfairness and the challenges.

It can be easy to assume that other people are the source of life's unfairness. It seems obvious that things such as racism, greed, sexism, lust for power and other human shortcomings are what cause life's unfairness, and that if we could just get rid of all that unfair, abusive behavior, life would be rich and fulfilling for everyone. Certainly greed and racism and all the rest do exist and can cause great harm to many people. Yet those things are not the source of life's unfairness. Even if we were to end them completely we would not end the unfairness in life.

If you believe that all of life's unfairness and troubles are caused by other people, consider this. Think about how it would be if you were dropped off in the most remote part of the Amazon jungle, hundreds of miles from the nearest person, completely out of the influence of other people. Would you still face challenges? Would life still be unfair? Consider how it would be if you were there completely naked and unequipped, with no clothes, no shoes, no map or compass or GPS device or satellite phone, no food, no water, no matches or lighter, and without even a container that you could fill with water. In other words, you would be completely free from all the unfairness imposed upon life by imperfect, self-serving people. What would you do? How long would you last? Do you think you would continue to encounter any unfairness? What if you came across a hungry jaguar, or an angry boar? What if a tiny insect bit you and infected you with malaria?

In such a scenario you would be completely free from the self-serving, unfair influences of other people. But here's the problem. You would also have to do without all the resources and benefits provided by those very same, self-serving influences. It is generally warm in the jungle so you might be okay without any clothes, though certainly not particularly comfortable. But it sure would be helpful to have a good pair of hiking boots. Have you ever thought about where hiking boots come from? They are manufactured by companies that are in business to make a profit. Hiking boots don't just fall from the sky. You can't just dig them up out of the ground. In order for you to have a good, comfortable pair of hiking boots, someone must make them. The people who make hiking boots don't do it just to be nice. They manufacture those boots as a way to make a profit, and ultimately as a way to support their own dreams. Yes, it may indeed be unfair that some people make a profit by producing hiking boots, and yes, it is certainly self-serving on the part of boot manufacturers to make that profit from their activities. But without that unfairness and without that profit, there would be no hiking boots.

But what if people could be convinced to make shoes and then give them away for free? Wouldn't that be better than having to pay for them? Wouldn't that take all the greed and unfairness out of the process? Or perhaps shoes could be sold at cost, with no profit, with the price set at just the right amount to pay the workers.

The problem is, no one would have the incentive to start such a business. No one would have the incentive to invest in such a business. No one would have any incentive to manage or grow such an enterprise.

There is a very well known business that does in fact give away millions and millions of pairs of shoes, Tom's Shoes. On a visit to Argentina in 2006, Blake Mycoskie encountered many children who had no shoes. He was inspired to start a company that would donate a pair of shoes to a child in need every time someone purchased a pair of shoes. The next year, he was back in Argentina with 10,000 pairs of shoes to donate to children. Within a few years, the company had given away more than a million pairs of shoes. For the children who receive them, the shoes are a life-changing event. It was all because one man had one dream.

It is wonderful that Tom's Shoes is able to give so many shoes to so many children in need. How are they able to do that? Because they make a profit. Profit keeps the company in business. The pursuit of profit motivates the people who run the company to continue coming up with stylish new designs. Profit enables the employees to earn a living. And profit pays to produce all those shoes that are given away for free. If the company stopped making a profit, they would eventually go out of business and there would be no more free shoes for children.

Life is not fair. It's not fair that Bill Gates has made billions of dollars by developing software for computers, or that Steve Jobs has made billions of dollars with Apple Computer, or that Sergey Brin and Larry Page have made billions of dollars by starting Google, while so many people can't even afford a place to live. It's not fair, and yet it's a whole lot better than the alternative. In the interest of fairness, would you be willing to give up your computer or the software that runs it? Would you be willing to do without the Internet or search engines like Google? The fact is, unfairness creates great progress that benefits us all.

Life is unfair, but so what? There's nothing that can be done to eliminate the unfairness, yet there's plenty that can be done to thrive and prosper in spite of it, and even because of it.

The Power of Ten Billion Dreams

Help Yourself First

Nature suffers nothing to remain in her kingdoms which cannot help itself.

— Ralph Waldo Emerson

It's great to help others achieve their dreams. Yet to do that, you must first begin to follow your own dreams. In the pre-flight speech that is given on every airline flight, the flight attendant instructs passengers what to do if the cabin loses pressure and oxygen masks drop from overhead. You've heard it dozens, maybe hundreds of times. Put on your own mask before you attempt to help someone else. Why? Because you can't help anyone else unless you are conscious. If you pass out from lack of oxygen while you're trying to help everyone else first, you're useless to anyone. In the same way, if you're not following your very own dream, you cannot effectively assist others in following their dreams. Put on your own oxygen mask first, and then you're in a position to be of assistance. Focus on connecting to and living your own dreams. That is what will put you in the best position to create value for many, many others in this world.

One dream I've always had is to be a writer, and to have my writing published. I love the written word and the ability of writing to add something of positive value to people's lives. Obviously, I've achieved that dream to a good degree, though it is something I never stop working on. I'm certainly humbled and honored to know that millions of people all over the world have enjoyed and benefited from the things I've written. Knowing that my writing makes a difference for people is without a doubt the main thing that keeps me doing it. And yet it is also very important that my writing makes a positive difference in my own life. It is the way I earn my living, and that is a big deal. Because that's what makes it sustainable. If I were not earning money from my writing, I would not be able to devote as much time and thought to it as I now do.

When I was just a kid, I started publishing. I produced a

neighborhood newspaper that I called *The Neighborly News*. In high school, I wrote articles for an "underground" newspaper on controversial social issues at the school. In college I published the weekly newsletter for my fraternity, the Delta Mu Chapter of the Sigma Chi Fraternity at Southern Methodist University. The weekly newsletter was a satirical send up of the things going on in the chapter. I loved the fact that all my fraternity brothers looked forward to the Monday evening chapter dinner when the *Delta Mu Tootsie* would be distributed. People would complain to me if I failed to make fun of them in the articles I wrote.

Looking back, I should have realized at the time that I had a future as a writer. But in 1976, when I graduated from college, I never really considered writing as a way to earn a living. I dabbled in writing a little bit, but mostly for my own enjoyment.

What's interesting is that even though I did not work as a writer for many years, the jobs I had were always closely connected to writing. Either I was working in a job that was connected with publishing, or I was finding a way to incorporate writing into my work. In high school I had a job delivering *The Dallas Morning News* every morning, a job that instilled in me the discipline I still call upon to come up with a new, original message for *The Daily Motivator* each day. My first job out of college was with a company that sold products to the printing industry. After that, I worked selling equipment and materials to computer chip manufacturers and other high tech businesses. In that job, I made a practice of writing extensive sales reports. In fact, I probably focused more on writing the reports than on making the sales calls. Later, I started my own business doing layout and design of publications. Of course that work was closely connected to writing and writers, and I loved it. That business eventually transformed into writing and publishing *The Daily Motivator* on the web.

The whole journey, from *The Neighborly News* to *The Daily Motivator* was fueled by my dream to write. Looking back on it, that's easy to see. As it was happening, though, it wasn't as obvious. There were, however, times when the dream broke through to the surface. I remember making a trip with my wife, Karen, to Key West, Florida in 1986. We toured the house where Ernest Hemingway lived and wrote during his Key West years, and saw some of the famous six-toed cats that were descended from Hemingway's pets. Standing out by Hemingway's swimming pool, which had been excavated out of the island's coral ground, under the lush tropical landscaping, I fell in love with the thought of being a writer. My dream of being a writer, which had been dancing around the edges of my life since I was a child, was starting to take hold. Now, as I write this, I'm sitting out by my own backyard swimming pool, surrounded by lush vegetation, and living the dream. In fact, as I'm committing these very words to paper (or the electronic equivalent on my Mac laptop), I'm realizing for the very first time how that experience of standing beside Ernest Hemingway's swimming pool provided some of the passion and energy that has enabled me to be sitting by my own pool, doing what I've always dreamed of doing.

Now, the colorful and unique city of Key West is connected to my new dream of sailing to Barbados, because it will definitely be a major stop along the way. In fact, a couple of months before my new dream was born, I traveled across the ocean from Texas to Key West, but it was in a 1000-foot cruise ship rather than a 40-foot sailboat. Even so, I can now look back and realize that my new dream was already calling to me by leading me to that trip.

In the fall of 1995 I started writing *The Daily Motivator* and publishing it on the web. Back then, only a small percentage of people even knew what the web was. Even so, the daily motivational messages quickly found a loyal following. Originally the messages were just a small part of another website, and served to provide some useful content that was updated each day. Within a few months, though, it was clear that *The Daily Motivator* had taken on a life of its own and was becoming far more popular than the rest of the site of which it was a part.

When I first started writing the messages, I intended to make them available for free on the web, and never really entertained the thought of charging for them. However, in the spring of 1996, a lot of people started asking if they could receive the daily messages by email. Many of them also mentioned that they would be willing to pay for the convenience of getting them that way. Suddenly I realized that I might have stumbled into a way to earn money from my writing. In June 1996 I began selling email subscriptions to *The Daily Motivator*. I continued to offer the same messages every day on the web for free, and I still do to this day. But for those who wanted to receive them by email, I began selling subscriptions for $15.00 a year, and still do.

In doing so, I learned a very important lesson about providing value to other people. I learned that in order to truly provide value to others, and to do so in the most effective and sustainable way, you have to make sure you receive value in return. Back in 1995 I had started writing *The Daily Motivator* basically as a hobby, just because the subject of personal development and the newly emerging web were things that interested me very much. I realize now that if it had remained just a hobby I would have stopped doing it a long time ago. At some point I would have lost interest or gotten sidetracked by something else, and the daily writing would have stopped. Yes, I know I would have certainly continued to write, because writing is such a passion of mine. But that writing would have taken other forms.

The reason *The Daily Motivator* has been around now for 15 years and is still going strong, is because I started charging that small $15.00 per year subscription price. I started receiving value in return for my writing, and that value has served over all these years to sustain *The Daily Motivator,* to expose the positive messages to more and more people every day.

At first, the subscriptions did not bring in much revenue, maybe a couple of hundred dollars a month. But that revenue grew, sometimes steadily and other times in spurts. Within about five years, The Daily Motivator was earning me a very good full-time income.

I'm relating this story not to boast about my success, but rather to illustrate a point. By charging for subscriptions, I was putting on my oxygen mask first. Yes, I absolutely wanted to be of service to others, and to provide something of real, life-changing value. But in order to help others in a powerful and sustainable way, I had to make sure I was helping myself first. That wasn't selfish. Selfish would have been for me to just write for my own amusement and to never make the work available for anyone else to read. Ironically, selfish would have been to refuse to make money from my writing, because doing so would have ensured that few people would ever have seen it.

Occasionally I receive emails from people who scold me for having the audacity to make money from my work. They tell me that if I was really interested in helping others, I would give away subscriptions for free. But I know better. I know that I could not afford the thousands of dollars per month in operating costs if I were giving away subscriptions for free. I might could have paid for the computers, software, servers and bandwidth for a couple of years out of my own pocket, but eventually my own funds would have run out, and then nobody would be reading *The Daily Motivator.*

There's something else I learned when I started charging for subscriptions. People receive much, much more value from the things they pay for than from the things they get for free. By charging a subscription price for *The Daily Motivator* emails, I'm giving subscribers a way to make an investment in their own personal development. Those who make that investment unquestionably get much more value out of the daily messages than those who don't.

There are a lot of people in this world who are living in desperate situations, and there are plenty of well-meaning people who want to help their fellow travelers on this journey of life. The desire to be of service to others is truly a beautiful thing. Yet in the zeal to offer value to others, it is important to remember that value only flows when it flows in both directions. You cannot give real value if you don't receive value in return. Yes, it might make you feel good and generous to give five dollars to a homeless person on the street, but you're not giving that person anything of lasting value that is going to improve his situation. If, on the other hand, you offer to pay him ten dollars to rake the leaves in your yard, that's a whole different situation. You're giving him the opportunity to earn some money and some self respect, you're giving him experience in being responsible and self sufficient. That's real value that can continue to positively impact his life long after the ten dollars is spent. And the way you provide that value is by getting your leaves raked in return for the money you pay—receiving value in return for value.

By the same token, you cannot expect to receive value from others unless you are willing to provide real, substantive value in return. Seeking to get something for nothing is demeaning to your self esteem, frustrating, and a losing proposition. When the oxygen masks fall from the ceiling, you better be prepared to put yours on yourself. Maybe someone will come along to put yours on for you, but don't count on it. Even if someone does put your mask on for you, it is still up to you to do the breathing. The meaningful value in your life is equal to the value you're willing to create.

This is certainly true when following your dreams. It is simply not going to do you any good if you expect someone else to fulfill your dream for you. What you get will not be what you wanted. What you get will be resentment and unhealthy dependency. Your dreams are yours for a reason. Those dreams are yours precisely so you can experience the fulfillment of making them real. You won't find fulfillment by living someone else's dream. You won't find fulfillment by getting someone else to achieve your dream for you.

The fact that you must make your own way in life is not a punishment. It is a privilege. Yes, it can be very difficult and even painful to be responsible for your own life and for your own dreams. Yet without that responsibility, there is no true richness. When you were a child, what was the thing you wanted more than anything else? You desperately wanted to be your own person. That's why you learned to walk on your own, and talk for yourself, and later to cross the street by yourself, and to choose your own friends and countless other things. You know deep inside that you are a unique expression of the magnificence of life, and the beautiful dream within you longs to take full responsibility for that expression. Anything short of that, and the dreamer will find no real fulfillment.

Life is beautiful when it is shared. Yet in order to share, you must maintain your own unique identity. Otherwise you have nothing to share, no value to give. And in order to receive value from others, you must respect that value by offering value in return.

Imagine yourself once again in the Amazon jungle, naked, with no shoes, no tools, no food or clean water. Feel the extreme difficulty and unfairness of life. Then look around at where you really are right now. You may not be ensconced in a penthouse suite at the Bellagio, but you're certainly better off than if you were alone in the jungle. And why exactly are you better off? What powerful force has provided you with the good and useful things you experience in spite of life's difficulty and unfairness? That force is the power of dreams to create real value. Because dreams have inspired the creation of value, and because individual dreamers have taken the responsibility to exchange value for other value, it has all led to a highly advanced lifestyle, a lifestyle that could not have even begun to be imagined by a villager living hundreds of years ago in the Amazon jungle. Such a world, built on dreams, is your extremely valuable legacy. And now you have the good fortune of adding the value of your own dreams to it.

The Power of Ten Billion Dreams

Is It Selfish To Dream?

If you were meant to cure cancer or write a symphony or crack cold fusion and you don't do it, you not only hurt yourself, even destroy yourself. You hurt your children.
You hurt me. You hurt the planet.

— Steven Pressfield

Is your dream selfish? Is it selfish to seek a life of fulfillment and joy, when so many other people live in poverty and pain?

You are, by nature, compassionate. You care about other people. You love the world where you live and you would love to live in a world where everyone experiences the joy of a full and rich life. So how do you bring that world into being? What can you do to help others enjoy lives of fulfillment?

Perhaps you could come up with a magnificent, ambitious plan to collect donations from wealthy people, and use those donations to help other people who are not as fortunate. But what would happen when the money was all spent, and the wealthy people didn't feel like giving any more, and the less fortunate people needed additional help? Though things might have been better for a little while, it didn't last very long.

Your dream matters. Every dream matters. People are not sustainably lifted up by government programs, as ambitious and extensive and well-funded as those programs might be. People are not sustainably lifted up by clever products, as useful as those products might be. People are not sustainably lifted up by charity, as compassionate as it may be. People are sustainably lifted up by their own dreams.

There was a time, when you were just a toddler, that you dreamed of intimately understanding those around you, and of making yourself clearly understood. That dream dominated your awareness. You devoted a large part of your time and energy, your thoughts and actions to the fulfillment of that dream. As you did, it gradually and steadily began to come true. After years of following that dream, you became wonderfully proficient at using language to richly communicate with those around you. From your dream to connect, you learned to talk and to understand what others were saying, and then you learned to used those language skills in written form through reading and writing.

Why did you have that dream and why did you follow it with such passion and persistence? You followed your dream of acquiring language skills—learning to talk, and then to read and write—because you felt the compelling urge to express yourself. You also had the desire to raise your experience of life to a new dimension by more fully understanding the experiences of others.

Since then you've had many more dreams. Every one of those dreams has revolved around something you wanted to experience about life, or something you wanted to express about yourself, or both. Even dreams that on their surface have not really benefited you directly, still have been about your desire for expression and experience.

Looking back on the dreams you've followed, there's something else they all share in common. It's something that applies equally to the dreams you've successfully crafted into reality, to the ones that are only partially fulfilled, and even to the dreams that you long ago abandoned. The efforts you've put into reaching each one of those dreams have brought value not only to your own life, but also to other lives as well. Even the most selfless dreams have been ways for you to express yourself and to feel certain desirable feelings. And even the most selfish dreams have brought value to the world beyond yourself.

If you could go on a worldwide television broadcast and say anything you wanted to hundreds of millions of people, what would you say? By following your dreams, you can say exactly the same thing, in an even more profound and influential way. When you talk, you speak with words. When you dream, and you follow those dreams, you speak with the power of a life well lived.

So, what is selfish and what is not? The most selfless thing you can do, is to make the most of yourself.

No, it's not selfish to follow your dream. What's selfish

is to stoke your ego by pretending that you're somehow saving the world by not taking more than your fair share. What's selfish is to feed your envy by criticizing those who build and create and achieve, and to claim that they're somehow selfish and self serving. What's selfish is to let your unique value stay locked inside of you because you're afraid of making waves. That's what is selfish.

What's compassionate, and caring, and altruistic, is to achieve. What helps others more than anything else is for you to go to work in the service of your most treasured dream. Because your achievements are not just yours. That's impossible. They cannot be. Your achievements benefit all of life.

If I were to have a magnificent, 8,500 square foot mansion built, that would seem like a very self-serving endeavor. Yet, that endeavor would accrue to the benefit of countless people. Of course the contractor and construction workers would benefit, but that's just the beginning. The house would need fixtures, furniture, electricity, appliances, an HVAC system, chemicals for the pool, an intrusion alarm with monthly monitoring, cable television and internet service, carpet, flooring and much more. People all over the world, making those products and providing those services, would benefit from having gainful employment.

Think about someone who earns 10 million dollars a year. That sounds like a lot, and it is. For the purpose of this example, it doesn't really matter how the person makes the money. Instead, let's look at what she can do with this money. Basically, she has just a few general choices. She can spend it. She can invest it. She can give it away. She can put it in the bank. What do all these choices have in common? They all benefit other people. There is nothing she can do with the money that won't benefit other people.

Contrast that with someone who does not make any money. His choices are different. He can beg for food and shelter and clothes and other necessities of life. He can borrow (though he has no way to pay it back). Or he can steal. How does any of that benefit anyone? Yes, he does have one other choice. He can go to work. Only if he chooses to do that, will he benefit others as well as benefitting himself. And, he starts to make some money.

Do you see a correlation here? The person who earns money has to do something of value for others to make that money in the first place, and then continues to benefit others no matter what is done with the money. The person who makes no money is most likely not contributing anything of value to anyone. That doesn't mean he or she is worthless as a person. It just means that earning money is more about giving than it is about taking.

Those relatively few people who have amassed fortunes worth billions of dollars are often urged to "give back" some of their good fortune to society through charitable activities and foundations. Indeed, many of those people don't need any prodding—they very willingly give in all sorts of different ways, which is wonderful. Yet in order to truly give back, they would had to have taken something in the first place, which they have not. They earned their fortunes by creating value for many, many other people. If they had not created all that value for other people, they would not have made all that money. It's great they want to use their wealth to benefit others. But it's not giving back. It is giving more. In fact, even those multi-millionaires and billionaires who don't give a cent to charity, still benefit many others with their wealth through their spending and investment.

The bottom line is this. When value is created by anybody, it can benefit everybody. It's not selfish to make a lot of money. It's not even selfish to live a lavish lifestyle if you've earned the wealth to support that lifestyle. Yes, it may be very narcissistic and foolish, but it's not selfish. It's not selfish to accumulate as much money or other wealth as you can possibly accumulate, as long as you're not stealing it. It's definitely not selfish to live the most extraordinary dream you can imagine.

So what is selfish? What's truly selfish is to let all your unique value stay hidden within you. What's selfish is to not create great value, to not become fantastically wealthy when you are fully capable of doing so. What's selfish is to expect something for nothing, to watch others create magnificent value, and expect them to give it to you just because life has been so unfair to you.

The Power of Ten Billion Dreams

What's selfish is to deny your dreams. Don't be selfish.

Asking yourself what you truly desire, and taking the time and making the effort to find an honest and meaningful answer, is one of the most compassionate, selfless, giving things you can do. Because asking that question, and knowing what you truly desire and why, will enable you to create great value, value that will extend far beyond our own life. Following your authentic desires is not selfish. It is the opposite. It is your way of making a real difference in he world. Stop feeling guilty about what you want to have, what you want to do, where you want to go, what you want to experience, how you want to live, the things you want to see, the things you want to accomplish. Let go of every last drop of guilt. And make your dreams come true. Make those things you desire happen. For in making them happen you make the world a better place.

The Power of Ten Billion Dreams

Dreams and Value

What is a cynic? A man who knows the price of everything and the value of nothing.

— Oscar Wilde

Here's a question that should be very easy to answer. Would you rather have a job that pays you $2,500 a month or $60,000 a month? Giving in to your fears and anxieties and looking for some way to just get by, might get you the $2,500, if you are lucky. Choosing to step confidently ahead and live your dream will get you the $60,000, or $600,000, or whatever you truly desire to experience in life.

Your life is an immense storehouse of potential value. A very small fraction of that value comes from the things you're able to do. You can tap into that little measly bit of value by trading your time for money in a job, for example. The vast majority of your potential value, however, comes from who you are deep inside. It is so valuable because it is absolutely authentic and unique. There is a big part of you that is like no one else who has ever lived. In that part of you is immense value, literally million-dollar value.

Why do you think certain singers make millions of dollars and others are lucky to get a few people to pay attention to them at the karaoke bar? There's an incremental difference in talent, to be sure, but that's not what distinguishes a million-dollar performer. The million-dollar performer is allowing her uniqueness to come through in her singing. The million-dollar athlete can indeed be a great team player, yet his most valuable moves come from his own unique essence. What is the unique essence within you? That's what your dreams will connect you with. How do you tap into the unique essence that holds more value than you could ever use in your lifetime? By living your dreams.

Following a dream is all about creating value. What is value? That's an excellent question. Answering that question can change your whole way of thinking about how the world works, and about how you can begin to live your dream the moment you choose to do so.

We often think of value in terms of money, so much so that we use the terms interchangeably. But value and money are not the same things. Yes, money has value in most cases (there are times when it doesn't), yet there is much more to value than money.

The dictionary defines value as the usefulness, importance or preciousness of something, and as a quality that causes things to be held in high regard. I prefer to think of value as anything that adds to the richness of life. In that sense, money can be valuable, but only when you're able to exchange it for other things. If, for example, you had a lot of money but were marooned on a remote island, that money would have no value to you. Your own personal memories have great value. You wouldn't want to be without them. Yet you probably could not sell them for money. Or could you? Perhaps if you wrote a memoir book you may indeed be able to transform the value of your personal memories into money. Love, experience, comfort and humor have great value, though they are not generally bought or sold as such. So value and money are definitely two different things, and that's a critical distinction to make.

Money has value only to the extent that you can exchange it for something of value to you. It has no intrinsic value but is instead a way to represent value. Think about the number 5. What could you buy with the number 5? Well, nothing. But what if that number 5 was used to represent the balance of your bank account? Then, you could purchase something with it, maybe a fast-food lunch. If there were several copies of the number 5 in your bank account, such as 55,555, you could buy a new car and have money left over. The number 5 itself won't get you anything, but when it represents the balance of your bank account, perhaps combined with other numbers, then you have something of value. Money itself is the same way. On its own, it has no value. But because it represents value that you've already created and exchanged for that money, then the money can be again exchanged for some other form of value. Money, then, is a very workable way of storing and exchanging value.

Our consumer society revolves around money, and because of that we tend to think of nearly everything in terms of money. That's understandable, and yet it is also very limiting. Why? Because you can't (legally) create money, but you can create value. When you focus so intently on getting money, you're focusing on something that is one step removed from what you're actually able to do. You are magnificently capable of creating great value, and you can almost always exchange that value for money in some way. But when you focus just on the money, and on your desire for it or your need for it, you overlook the whole realm of real value that you can create.

Following a dream is not about making money. If making money is your dream, I suggest you do some more work on that dream. Dig deeper. It's not the money you really dream about. It's what you can buy with the money. It's what the money will enable you to experience. On the other side of the equation, you're not really going to be able to make any money directly. What you can do is create value and then exchange that value for money.

Once, you were a baby. You couldn't walk or even crawl. You just had to stay where they put you. You would be situated in one place, and you could see another place that looked very interesting and enticing, and you wanted to be there. But you just weren't able to get yourself there. As much as you wanted to be there, it wasn't happening. That was completely frustrating.

So you did the only thing you knew how to do. You cried. And maybe some of those times when you cried, someone came and lifted you up and took you to the place where you wanted to be. But it wasn't a reliable strategy, because other times when you cried you would be taken somewhere you didn't want to go. In your frustration, you desperately searched for other options. And you found them. You learned to crawl, and then to walk. And with the crawling and the walking, you were finally able to get yourself where you wanted to be.

Now that you're all grown up and you want to make money, you face a similar dilemma. You know you want to have a lot of money, but the desire alone is not enough to get you that money. You can wish and hope, and even cry and whine, and maybe every now and then a little money will come your way, but it's not a reliable strategy. Because you're assuming that somebody else has to give it to you. What you have to do is similar to learning to walk. You have to create a workable strategy that will take you from where you are now, using what is already available to you, to the money you wish to have, and then to the things that money will buy. That strategy is to create value. If you focus just on the money, all you'll end up doing is crying, just like when the baby you focused only on where you wanted to be. However, when you turn your attention toward creating value, you'll discover that you can make as much money as you wish to make, just like when you finally learned to walk you were able to go almost anywhere you could then imagine.

When it comes to money, there are two things vital to keep in mind. The first is that you don't really desire to have money—your desire is for what that money can buy. The second is that you cannot make money directly—you must create value and then exchange that value for money. Coming and going, money is nothing more than an intermediate step. In the end, value is what really counts. Meaningful value is what will add richness to your life. Value is what enables you to experience what you want to experience. Value is what you desire and what you're able to create.

So how do you do that? How do you create value? There's really no limit to the ways you can create value. Creating value is a highly personal thing. Some people are better at creating certain kinds of value, and other people are better at creating other kinds of value. That, by the way, is why the use of money has become so widespread. Money, along with a free and vibrant marketplace, enables you to create the kind of value that you're most skilled at creating, and to exchange that value for money, and then to exchange money for just about any kind of value you can imagine to desire, including value that you really want to have but cannot even begin to know how to create. I am skilled at writing, but I know very little about how to get oil out of the ground and refine it into gasoline. So I write a book or a motivational newsletter, get paid for it with money, and use that money to buy gasoline, which is produced by people who know much more about that kind of stuff than I ever will.

Thinking in terms of value will empower you. Seeing life in terms of value creation is a key element of following your dreams. Because a dream is in fact an intention to create and experience a very specific form of value. To reach that dream is to create value.

Actually, you are creating value all the time. Every moment of every day, you are creating the value that keeps you alive and that keeps your world going. There is a limitless abundance surrounding you. With your thoughts and actions, you focus that abundance toward some particular ends. You breathe in air, and it delivers the nourishing value of oxygen to your cells. You observe life's beauty, and create a beautiful painting that brings pleasure to others. Your life is a continuing experience of value creation and expression.

Following your dreams and achieving those dreams requires nothing more, in general, than what you're already doing, which is creating value. The main difference is that instead of maintaining your value-creating focus for a few minutes or a few hours, your dreams ask that you stay focused on them for much longer periods of time. Sometimes it's even for a whole lifetime. But other than the time frame of your focus, achieving your dreams is no different than what you're already doing on a daily basis. In fact, you already know ninety-five percent of what you must know how to do in order to reach any dream you can imagine. That's because what you must know is how to think and how to act, and you've been doing those things all your life.

To reach your dreams is to express new value in a new and meaningful way. And what is the raw material you use to create that value? You tap into the limitless abundance in which your life is immersed. Just by virtue of being alive and aware, you are capable of accessing that abundance. Much of the value you create comes from making use of value that is already available to you. There is great wealth already in your life. Where do you find it? You'll find it in just about everything you do.

Consider the things that interest you, and the knowledge you have. What things are you just naturally curious about?

You possess a great deal of valuable information on those subjects, whatever they may be. It is information that could be of great use to others. When you become intimately familiar with a particular subject, it's natural to assume that most other people are just as knowledgeable. Of course they are not. Many of the things you know about your favorite subjects could be put to good use by others, if you made it available to them in some way. Do you have knowledge of specific processes, industries, disciplines, situations, machines, people, history, or places? That knowledge can be highly valuable. Browsing though a bookstore will show you that people, on a daily basis, pay money in order to obtain knowledge. Your specialized knowledge is indeed quite valuable.

Your character is extremely valuable. If you are dependable, honest, forthright, disciplined and compassionate, those are all qualities that are highly valued by other people. In a later chapter we'll look at how extremely valuable integrity is. Your character is valuable not only to your family and your employer. It is potentially valuable in almost anything you undertake. Consider the value of character if you were to run for elected office, seek financing for an entrepreneurial venture, adopt a child, become a role model for others, or solicit customers for your business.

Your skills are another abundant source of value. In going through life, you have learned to do many things. You have specific skills, such as operating a particular software program. You also have more generalized skills, such as being able to recognize business opportunities. Both types of skills are valuable, and they can be used to create a continuing stream of value in your life. Recognize your skills as a valuable part of your life, build them and improve on them, and by all means use them to their fullest extent.

Your family can provide you with support, encouragement, fulfillment, and a secure, loving environment. These are extremely valuable, no matter what you are doing. This is a source of value that many people take for granted until they lose it.

Your experience is quite valuable. Think of the first day you spent working at your current job. How effective were

The Power of Ten Billion Dreams

you? How much did you get done? Probably not very much—you were too busy figuring out how to do everything. Consider how much more effective you were after the first month, or the first year. That is the value of experience. Your experience in life goes way beyond your job. Perhaps you have traveled, bought a home, maintained an automobile, cared for an elderly relative, formed a bowling league, served on your church's finance committee. All these experiences have great value that can be transferred to other pursuits.

There is much value to be found in the people you know. Not only do you have access to the people you know, you also have access to the people they know, and the people they know, and so on. All of these people have value in their own right, and can add significant value to your life.

Also highly valuable are your insight, your opinions, your special perspective on life, your sense of humor, your appreciation for beauty and art. Think of all the ways in which these qualities could permit you to create value for yourself and others. You probably take them for granted, but they are extremely valuable, particularly when coupled with your unique perspective.

Finally, you can find much hidden wealth in the problems you have had. Think about it. If you were going into, say, the restaurant business, would it be worthwhile to talk at length with someone who had failed in the same business? You bet it would. Just think what you would learn from such a person. Similarly, a recovering alcoholic or former drug abuser can very effectively encourage young people to stay away from drugs. That's an extremely valuable skill.

In the same way, the problems that you have faced are of great value to yourself and others. You've learned what not to do. You have a very good idea of how to prevent the same problems from occurring again. Your negative experience has taught you many valuable positive lessons.

So really, everything you have done, all that you are, all that you know, and even the problems and pains contribute real value to your life. Combine that with a dream that is authentically you, and there is within you the power to add immense richness to your world.

Your job is to do just that. Your job is to take that dream, immerse it in the value that's already yours, then step forward and create the new value that will make that dream a reality. You're not just out to make money. You're making something real and meaningful. You're creating value that will positively impact not just your life but countless other lives around you.

The value you create can be something that benefits your life directly, such as building a patio in your back yard, or it can be something that you provide to someone else in exchange for other value, such as working at a job where you earn money. When you're exchanging value, there's something important to remember. In order for anyone (including you) to benefit from the value you provide to others, you must receive equivalent value in return. This can be money, or prestige, or a sense of accomplishment—whatever you want it to be. It is crucial to the whole process that you receive value in exchange for the value you provide.

Management consultant Peter Drucker was once asked by *Forbes Magazine* how much he charged for his consultation services. His answer: "If you don't charge enough money that they are conscious of it, you have no impact." So basically he was saying that if people don't sacrifice something to get his advice, then they don't benefit from the advice. That is an important lesson.

When you create value for others, the most responsible thing to do is to exchange it for other value. People simply don't value or benefit from things unless they have paid the price for them. In fact, it is the price (monetary or otherwise) that conveys much of the sense of value. When conveying value, you want to convey it intact. And that means you are obligated to make sure it is as valuable to the person receiving it as it is to you. The way to do that is to make sure you receive sufficient value in return. Otherwise, the value you have given is drained. Value only exists to the extent that it is upheld by the person possessing it. The only responsible and effective way to convey value is to exchange it for equivalent value.

Living your dream, then, is all about creating value in your own unique way, and exchanging that value for other value if you choose. The possibilities for doing so are truly unlimited.

The Power
of Self-Interest

That which is common to the greatest number has the least care bestowed upon it.

— Aristotle

Over the last couple of hundred years, and in particular during the last thirty years or so, our human civilization has sustained a phenomenally high level of achievement, in spite of the obstacles. Hundreds of millions of people have been lifted out of poverty into lives of greater quality, comfort and fulfillment. Millions and millions more have become, when compared to historical standards, truly rich. In many wealthy countries, even unskilled laborers are able to maintain lifestyles that would be envied by an 18th century monarch.

Yet there are enormous challenges that remain. People living outside wealthy, developed countries are still desperately poor. At the same time, many people and nations within the developed world have been living beyond their means and have accumulated burdensome debt. Add to that the challenge of providing food and energy and clothing and shelter and all the comforts of a modern lifestyle for billions of people without savaging the environment.

To keep up with the many challenges, the world requires an enormous amount of achievement, an enormous amount of value creation. And achievement comes from individuals who are free and who are motivated to follow their dreams. It doesn't happen because some government official issues a proclamation. It doesn't happen because some business executive demands it. Real, substantive achievement comes from individuals, each motivated by a dream that comes from genuine self-interest. Achievement comes from individuals, working cooperatively more often than not, each following their dreams by learning, working, taking the initiative and creating value. The massive amount of value creation the world so desperately requires will come from people who seek to follow their dreams through their own efforts, even if those dreams may appear to be completely self-serving. As Adam Smith observed, "It is not from the benevolence of the butcher, the brewer, or the baker that we expect our dinner, but from their regard to their own interest."

But are we really better off in a world where each person is motivated by his or her own personal dreams? Isn't that selfish and somehow immoral? Wouldn't it be better if everyone could be persuaded to work for the common good? Wouldn't that be more fair and just for everyone?

It has certainly been tried. The twentieth century was witness to perhaps the most horrible, destructive, brutal, murderous failure in human history—communism. As an economic strategy, communism very simply did not work. It sounded like a great idea on paper. When Karl Marx envisioned communism, he thought that by abolishing private property and ending class divisions, people would be free to achieve at maximum levels and would, in fact, produce an overwhelming abundance of goods and services. But he did not take into account the undeniable human yearning for freedom. He did not take into account the fact that when freedom is stifled, so are creativity and productivity. Communism depends on people doing as they are told. But people have a natural aversion against doing what they are told. People prefer to do what they choose. Every living creature naturally acts in its own self-interest, and humans are no different. That's not selfish. In fact it is highly responsible. It is a natural inclination that is responsible for our very survival. The failure of communism demonstrates what happens when political and economic systems oppose our natural inclination toward self-interest, even if those systems are devised with the best of intentions.

The failure of communism does not mean that there's anything inherently wrong about communal living, in which people agree to share the fruits of their collective efforts. The tragic error of communism was in the attempt to scale up the commune to massive proportions. In a small commune, everyone knows each other, and that familiarity reduces the potential for abuse. In a large communist nation, people who make the decisions are far removed from those who must live under those decisions, and such a system is ripe for abuse. Certainly communal arrangements have their place and can work very well, but only when all the members of the group participate by choice, and have direct input and influence over how it functions. So far that has proven to be impossible on a large scale. In fact, the desire of individuals to escape communism is so strong that many communist countries had to tightly seal their borders to keep citizens from fleeing. Before the Berlin Wall was constructed in 1961, more than three million people illegally defected from communist East Germany to the freedom of neighboring West Germany. Even after the wall was constructed, more than five thousand people attempted to escape over the 12-foot-high, heavily guarded barrier, with approximately 200 killed during their attempts.

For people who willingly choose it, communal living can indeed be personally fulfilling. Yet for larger, more widespread groups of people who don't all personally know each other, it is far more productive to respect, harness and utilize the desire of people to act in their own self-interest. That is the point made by Adam Smith. The butcher, the brewer and the baker practice their trades not because they're told to do so, but because they choose to do so in their own self-interest. They spend their time and use their resources to produce goods, which they can trade for other goods.

Adam Smith's model, the free market, is not perfect. However, it is arguably better than any other system anyone has come up with. That's because the free market was not designed by anyone. Instead, it just naturally happens when people are free to act in their own self-interest. It is not a planned situation, but rather an acknowledgment of human nature.

So, if the free market is such a natural state of affairs, and if it enables so much prosperity, why was anyone ever interested in something like communism? What is the appeal of a system that restrains people from acting in their own self-interest?

Communism was in large part a reaction to the Industrial Revolution of the 18th and 19th centuries. Before the Industrial Revolution, just about everything that people used or consumed was made by hand, using small tools. Energy was supplied primarily by human effort, draught animals, wind and flowing water. Then in the late 1700s, mechanization using steam engines began to transform the way things were produced and transported. Eventually this mechanization spread around the world and was responsible for massive increases in productivity. It dramatically raised living standards. Between 1800 and 2000, the world's average per-capita income increased more than 1,000 percent. That's a pretty amazing accomplishment, especially when you consider that the figure is for average income. People in the year 2000, on average, had 10 times as much material value available to them per year compared to people in 1800. And of course, by 2000 there were a whole lot more people than there were in 1800.

That's the good news about the Industrial Revolution. But there was bad news, too. With mechanization came a consolidation of production into large factories. These large production facilities required large investments of capital. The artisans of the 16th and 17th centuries, who used small tools and produced goods one at a time, were replaced by large factories using massive machines that could produce the same goods in high volume at a lower cost. For rich, well-connected people this was a fantastic opportunity. They could build large factories, employ minimally-skilled workers at low wages, crank out vast quantities of valuable products, and make a handsome profit selling those products at prices far below what similar handcrafted products might sell for. But for those who worked in the factories, the advantages of the Industrial Revolution were not as compelling. They were toiling their lives away in dirty, hot, smoky, loud, dangerous places while much of the value they produced was being pocketed by the factory owners. The situation was ripe for resentment, and communism appealed to that resentment.

Communism's big promise was that the workers would own the means of production. That sounded like a great arrangement to the workers. Instead of a capitalist factory owner reaping more of the benefits and profits from the factory's efficient production, the workers themselves would receive that value. Instead of a society composed of rich factory owners and poor workers, communism offered to deliver a socially just society in which everyone benefited equally from the goods and services that were produced. Based on that promise, communism spread, sometimes by peaceful means and many times by violent revolution, to all corners of the world.

But there are many serious flaws with communism, or any kind of forced collectivism. Chief among them is the absence of incentive. Think about it. If you're going to get paid the same amount no matter how much work you do, how much work will you do? If you're going to get paid the same whether you make an extra effort or not, how much extra effort will you make? Probably not much. Yet it is from that extra effort that achievement comes. It is from that extra effort that innovation comes. When people are discouraged from making an extra effort, their work stagnates and their productivity goes nowhere.

Another problem with communism is an absence of responsibility. When everybody owns the factory, then nobody owns it. When nobody owns it, nobody takes it upon himself or herself to maintain or upgrade the factory, or any other kinds of property for that matter. While it's true that private ownership of property can lead to significant inequities and abuses, that same private ownership also leads to responsibility. Ask yourself this. Are you as careful when driving a rental car as you are when you're driving your own car? Do you, for example, slow down for potholes in a rental car as readily as you would in your own car? If you're like most people, the answer is no. While you are certainly careful not to inflict any obvious damage to the rental car, you're probably not as careful when it comes to things that would cause long-term wear on the vehicle, such as gunning the engine, hard braking, and driving over speed bumps. And there's a very good, understandable reason for that. It's not your car and you won't have to pay for the long-term wear and tear. Besides, it's a rental car and everybody else is hard on it too, so there's really no advantage, even to the car itself, that comes from being careful with it.

With ownership comes responsibility, and when there is no ownership, there is simply very little incentive to be responsible. Drive through a neighborhood in your city where most of the houses are rental houses. Then drive through a neighborhood where most of the houses are occupied by their owners. Can you see a difference in the maintenance of the buildings, in the landscaping, in the cleanliness? The difference is one of ownership. Even a small, inexpensive home where the owner lives will usually be cleaner and better maintained than a bigger, pricier home that's rented to someone else by an owner who lives in another state.

The promise of communism is a society in which all citizens work for the common good, utilizing assets that are owned collectively by all. But just like all other living things, humans are hard-wired for survival, and that means putting their individual interests ahead of the interests of others. For communism to function, that natural self-interest must be opposed in many areas of life, by force if necessary, which is often the case. That's why as many as 100 million people have died under communism from starvation, politically-motivated murder and forced labor. And that's why many people who live under communism are eager to escape.

As long as people are naturally inclined to act in their own self-interest, it makes sense to structure society in such a way that respects and harnesses the power of self-interest in a positive and beneficial way. Sure, free market economies do indeed have many problems. Yet it is an indisputable fact that they create much more wealth and higher living standards than any alternative that has ever been tried.

In a free market economy, people are free to own property and to succeed or fail based on their own efforts. Each individual has a powerful incentive to be as productive as possible, and to be as responsible as possible. Obviously that is beneficial on an individual level, but is it really good for society to have all those people looking out only for themselves? Doesn't that encourage selfishness, create unfairness and lead to wide disparities in income and lifestyles?

Well, it turns out that in a truly free and transparent market, the best strategy for success is to create as much value as you can for as many other people as you can. That's the dynamic which has built the amazing worldwide achievement machine that we have today. In a free and transparent mar-

The Power of Ten Billion Dreams

ket, it is in your best interest to serve the interests of other people, because they will pay you handsomely for doing so. The baker wants people to buy his bread, so he makes it delicious with healthy ingredients. If the bread tasted awful, there would be another baker who, sensing an opportunity, would open a shop selling better-tasting bread and attract customers away from the original baker. If a butcher sold meat that made people sick, word would quickly spread and she would go out of business. In a truly free and transparent market, this all happens organically, without the need for official regulation. Merchants and manufacturers have an incentive to stay in business, because that's what provides them with their income. They know that to stay in business they must provide their customers with good, solid value, so they do everything within their power to make that happen. In this way, the natural impulse to look out for oneself is harnessed in a powerful and effective way to benefit all of society.

That all sounds great in theory, but we know from living in a (relatively) free market economy that it doesn't always work that way. Merchants often provide very poor customer service. Manufacturers regularly sell products that don't work very well. How does the marketplace allow this to happen? If the free market is such a good system, how are businesses able to take advantage of their customers and still stay in business?

The answer is that we do not live in a purely market-driven economy. There are all sorts of other factors that influence the economy. For various reasons we have chosen to put restraints on the free market. These restraints, though they are often implemented with the best of intentions, distort the functioning of the free market and often pave the way for abuses and other undesired consequences.

Many people, for example, are not satisfied with their cable television service. They consider the price too high, and find that the customer service is very poor. And yet, they continue to subscribe to their cable service. Why? Because there is no direct competition. In most cities, there is only one choice if you want to subscribe to cable television. There are some understandable reasons for this. For example, to deliver cable service to every home requires running wires throughout the city into every neighborhood. Those wires must run along or underneath the city's public streets, so city government officials must give permission for the installation of a cable network. It would be highly disruptive for a dozen competing cable companies to maintain separate, redundant networks of signal transmission lines all over town, so by municipal authority the town limits itself to just a single provider. As such, that provider has a captive audience. If you live in the town where they operate, you just have one choice. Either you pay what they charge, and you put up with their dismal customer service, or you are not able to watch cable television. Even though the cable company is a private enterprise, it is not really operating in a purely free market scenario. Thus they're able to get away with some level of abuse and still remain in business.

However, cable television is starting to get some very viable competition, and it will be interesting to see what happens to the business as the result of competitive forces. For example, it is now very easy to deliver high definition streaming video over the Internet, thus bypassing the cable companies. With most cable companies, television programming is sold as a package. For example, if you want to be able to watch the Food Network you may have to buy a premium package that includes 200 other channels you'll never watch. But Internet streaming makes it easy to sell and deliver individual channels, and even individual programs, on an a la carte basis. I expect that within a very short period of time, prices for cable television programming will become much more competitive, and options for selecting customized packages of just the channels you want will become common, due to the competition from Internet-based providers such as Hulu and Netflix.

That's how the amazing worldwide achievement machine grows more powerful, more effective and more accessible to more people—through competitive market forces. If something is way too unaffordable, some innovative person finds a way to make it more affordable. If some product or service is missing certain desired options, an entrepreneur steps up to offer those options. And each time it happens, there is a net benefit. Sure, those who just collect money without putting it back into innovation will eventually be driven out of business, but on the whole, everybody is better off because of the competition. Yes, that competition can seem brutal when you are on the losing end of it. But over time, and in a relentless way, it creates ever-increasing value for the world. It creates a world in which there are more and more possibilities and opportunities each day for living the life of your dreams.

But there is a serious threat to the amazing worldwide achievement machine. The machine is in place, it is accessible to more and more people each day, and yet far too many people fail to put it to use. Far too many people fail to understand the awesome power of their own dreams. Whether it is because of ignorance, guilt, resentment, arrogance, or some other factor, the amazing worldwide achievement machine is in danger of being compromised. People who could be highly productive, who could bring great richness to all of life, who could live their most treasured dreams, are, for one reason or another, being discouraged from doing so. Sometimes it is due to misplaced compassion. Other times, the motives are more sinister.

If left unchecked, that trend could seriously compromise or even destroy the amazing worldwide achievement machine, by slowly and surely eating away at it. If that were to happen, the world would not be a very nice place to live. In fact, it would be a dark, hopeless place, filled with despair, a hell on earth. Because not only have we built an amazing achievement machine, we depend on it. Do you grow the fruits and vegetables that you eat? Do you collect the water that you drink each day? Do you personally know anyone who does? Most likely, no, you don't. Most likely, you wouldn't even know where to begin if you had to provide, all on your own, your own food and water. And what about all the other things you depend on? If the oil or natural gas or electricity stopped coming, how would you heat your home? If the Internet and telephone network went dark, how would you stay connected with the people you care about? The achievement machine, run by millions and millions of individuals, each effectively and positively motivated by self-interest to be productive, brings you the necessities of life and the not-so-necessary things as well.

There is today a very real threat to our civilization, a civilization upon which billions of lives depend. That threat is not from natural disaster. That threat is not from violent war. That threat is not primarily physical in nature. One of the most disconcerting threats to our civilization is a simple, yet tragically mistaken assumption—the assumption that it is somehow wrong to be prosperous and successful and to follow your own dreams.

In fact, dreams are an absolute necessity. The amazing worldwide achievement machine is built on dreams, and depends on dreams to keep in running. Not only is it perfectly fine for you to act in your own self-interest and to follow your dreams, it is in the best interest of everyone else for you to do so.

My dream is to sail my own boat to Barbados. Why should anyone care? What difference will that make in the world? Well, let's look at the alternative. What if I did not have that dream? Without that dream, I would just continue along, doing what I do, writing *The Daily Motivator* each day, hopefully making enough money to pay the mortgage and insurance and grocery bills. In other words, I'd just be continuing along as I have been for the last few years. With the dream, however, things change. First and foremost, my dream of sailing to Barbados gave me the extra motivation and the overreaching concept necessary to finish this book and to get it published. As a result, many people will purchase copies of the book and some of them will be inspired by its message to live their own dreams. In the process of doing just that, a lot of other people will benefit. The book has to be printed, so people will earn money by printing it. The printed books also must be shipped to the people who purchase them, so that will provide a way for other people to earn money, including truck drivers, postal workers, aircraft pilots, the people who maintain the trucks and aircraft, and people who work in centers that process shipments.

So, what is frivolous and what is not? The fact is, my dream compels me to create value, and that value cannot help but spill over into the lives of others. Any dream that is positive and authentic will do the same.

No, it's not wrong to follow your dreams. In fact, the com-

The Power of Ten Billion Dreams

plete opposite is true. We have lifted ourselves to the point where it is not only perfectly fine to live a rich and fulfilling life, it has actually become something of a moral imperative. The bottom line is that you owe it to life to live your most authentic and treasured dreams.

Why have we delved so deeply into such prosaic subjects as economics and communism, free markets and competition, when this is a book about dreams? Because you are an essential steward of the amazing worldwide achievement machine. It is important that you understand and appreciate what a truly powerful thing it is. The amazing worldwide achievement machine is so amazing because it is not controlled by anyone. It was not planned or conceived by anyone. It rose up on the power of dreams, not any one dream but a whole world history full of dreams. And it has to have new dreams to keep going. If it breaks down, everyone is in big trouble, especially those who are already less fortunate.

If you love life, if you love your fellow human beings, if you love the beautiful planet on which you live, the best way you can express that love is by living your very own most authentic and treasured dreams.

And as good as it is to live a life of richness and fulfillment, there's something that's even better. What's even better is for everyone else to also experience the fulfillment that comes from living their dreams. Is that just some utopian fantasy? No, in many ways, for many people, it has actually happened. By comparison with, say, two hundred years ago, most of the people today in developed countries are indeed rich—far beyond anything their great-grandparents could have dared to dream. It's time that we fully realize how good we have it. It's time to understand how we can realistically lift ourselves even higher and by so doing, lift literally billions of other people out of poverty and into a rich, fulfilling life, a life driven by the power of ten billion dreams.

There is plenty of abundance in this world and in this universe for every person to be as rich as he or she chooses to be. There is plenty of abundance in this life for every person to live his or her most treasured and authentic dreams. And it all begins with you, choosing to live yours.

The Power of Ten Billion Dreams

The Power of
Ten Billion Dreams

Every challenge we face can be solved by a dream.
— David Schwartz

There is no single solution to the immense challenges faced by the world today. No amount of money, no amount of financial manipulation, no amount of intervention even by the most powerful governments, no grand plan crafted by the most highly educated and credentialed thinkers has the power to adequately address even a small fraction of our problems.

Even so, there is hope. In fact, it is an entirely realistic, workable and accessible hope. There is a power that can successfully and appropriately address not only the big, worldwide problems, but the small, individual ones as well. It is a power that can indeed be quickly and effectively applied in a countless variety of situations to bring real richness and fulfillment to life. It is a power we already possess, that needs no complicated development or implementation plan. Any person at any time can tap into this power simply by allowing it and then working to follow it.

It is the power of ten billion dreams. The way to activate that power is to give people all over the world the freedom and encouragement to pursue their very own dreams.

What's the best thing you can do for the world? What's the most significant contribution you can make to life? Do you even care about making a difference for other people, or are you more interested in following your own dream? Do you want to make a real difference in the world, or do you just want to have a good time and fully enjoy your own life? Be honest! When you wake up each morning, what's your first thought? Is it, "What can I do today to make the world a better place?" Or is it, "What would I really like to be doing right now?"

Or do you perhaps have every intention of making the

world a better place, but you're worried that if you put your focus in that direction that your own life, your own family and the dreams you have for yourself and your family will suffer as a result? After all, no one wants be a chump. If everyone else out there is looking out only for themselves, perhaps you should, too. Right?

Are you conflicted between your desire to make a positive difference in the world and your desire to follow your very own special dreams? Then here's some great news. There is absolutely no need for any conflict.

The best thing you can do for the world is to be successful at being you. The best thing you can do for all of life is to follow your authentic dreams with all the passion and energy you have. Your dreams are yours for a very good and worthwhile reason. Even if those dreams seem to have no bearing on anyone else, even if those dreams feel completely selfish, still they have the power to add great value to all of life.

Do you wish to help others? That's great! But you don't have to give up your own dreams to do so. The very best way you can help others is to bring your most authentic dreams to life.

You owe it to life to dream the biggest, most wonderful and meaningful dreams you can imagine. You owe it to life to achieve those dreams, to make them real. Your dreams are more than mere fleeting fantasies or elaborate wishes. In your most authentic dreams you'll find the essence of what you have to give to life. Those authentic dreams are profoundly intertwined with your true purpose. Those dreams define a pathway for you to express your purpose.

Even if you never donate money to charity or go on a mission trip or work serving meals to the homeless, you can help others immensely by living the life you dream of living. Maybe that dream includes going on mission trips or taking a vow of poverty or ministering to street people and if so, that's wonderful. But those explicitly charitable pursuits are not the only way to be of great service to others, not by a long shot. As long as your dream is authentic, as long as it is truly yours, as long as it is positive and joyful and fulfilling, it will enable you to move the world forward.

Perhaps your dream is to be one of the first space tourists. Or maybe your dream is to live in a 20-room mansion overlooking the Mediterranean Sea. Your dream might be to own a champion race horse, or to travel around the country in a recreational vehicle, or to work as an executive assistant or to sing on Broadway. No matter what that dream may be, as long as it is really yours it will move all of life forward.

The world is moved forward by dreams, and specifically, by individual dreams. Real, authentic dreams are intimate things. In order for a dream to have power, it must come from you. While you can certainly appreciate and admire the dreams of others, the only dreams that will push you forward are the dreams that come from within you. Martin Luther King, Jr. did not say "we have a dream." In his landmark speech on the steps of the Lincoln Memorial in 1963 he proclaimed "I have a dream." It was his dream and he explicitly said so. That dream inspired millions, and resonated with the dreams of countless others, yet it was his very own dream, coming from the depth of his essence, and that's what made it so powerful. Real dreams are not the result of marketing focus groups or congressional committee hearings. Real dreams come, one at a time, from real people.

Even if no one but you ever knows about your dream, as long as you follow it with passion and purposeful action, many, many others will benefit from it. Though they won't share your particular dream, they each have dreams of their own. When you follow your dream, you will, in very real ways, enable other people to follow their dreams. In the same way, when they follow their dreams it will enable still others to follow a whole additional set of dreams. And through the power of those dreams, the world is pushed forward.

So how exactly does that work? How can one person's dream be of value to other people if that person has no intention of helping others? A good way to understand is with some examples.

First, consider someone who gives away his all possessions to help the poor. Imagine that the person is a man who is worth ten million dollars. He decides to give it all away to help people who are less fortunate than himself. That would seem to be incredibly generous, but is it really the most generous thing he can do? Well, maybe not. Because once he gives away the ten million dollars, he is left with nothing more to give. Not only that, he then has no way to support himself and as a result he may very well become a burden on society.

Now, consider an alternative. Suppose that instead of giving away the ten million dollars, the person has a dream to own a car dealership. He puts all his money into launching the business. For a few years, the business requires all his time and money to get going, so he is unable to give anything to others. Or is he? Actually, by opening a business he is providing many people with the opportunity to work and to earn a living (and to follow their own dreams). There are the car salespeople, the office workers, the mechanics, customer service representatives, accountants, janitorial and building maintenance workers, and others who have good jobs because of the business he has created. And after a few years, the business starts generating profits, to the tune of about two million dollars a year in addition to paying the founder of the business a good income that can support him and his family. At that point, he can take the two million dollars profit each year and donate it to help those less fortunate than himself. The good thing about this scenario is that he can continue doing so indefinitely. Instead of running out after giving away just ten million dollars, he can continue giving away two million dollars every year for as long as he wishes to do so—all because instead of giving away that initial ten million dollars, he used it to build a profitable business.

So, which adds more value to the world—someone who gives away all his money or someone who uses that money to follow his dream?

For various reasons the term "profit" has come to have a negative connotation in polite society. Many people seem to think that anyone who earns a profit is being greedy and self-serving. But that is sheer nonsense! In reality, it is the other way around. What is profit, anyway? Profit represents value that is created. Let's say that again, because it is an absolutely essential concept. Profit represents value that is created. There's nothing shameful about creating value.

The Power of Ten Billion Dreams

Imagine that you buy a parcel of land, some concrete, some nails, some wood and brick and carpet and wires and pipes and paint for a total of $200,000. Then you put it all together and it becomes a home, which you sell to a family for $300,000. You've made a profit of $100,000, and that profit represents the difference in value between the raw materials and the finished home. You didn't steal that $100,000 from anyone. You didn't cheat anyone out of it by deceiving them or selling them something at a ridiculously inflated price. What you did was to create something of real, lasting value, for which a family was eager to pay the going market price. You took $200,000 worth of land and materials and made it into a $300,000 home.

Consider another example of profit—one that does not involve being paid in cash. Imagine that your son just left home to go to college, and you want to convert the room that was formerly his bedroom into a study. One thing you'll need is a nice desk. So you go out shopping for a desk. At one furniture store, you find an excellent desk that's just the right size. The store will deliver it, fully assembled, to your home for a total price of $1,500. That sounds reasonable. Then you go to another store and see exactly the same desk. At the second store, however, the price is only $800, a savings of $700. But there's a catch. If you buy it from the second store, it comes disassembled in a box. You'll have to pick it up at the store, carry it home, and put it together. But you're pretty handy with things like that, and the $700 difference in price is certainly substantial, so that's what you decide to do. You pay the $800, back your pickup truck up to the loading dock at the store and drive off with your new desk. When you get home, you carry all the pieces into your study and spend the next two hours putting everything together. When it's all done, you have a nice new desk that's just what you wanted. Instead of spending $1,500 on it, you spent just $800 and then put it together yourself. The difference of $700 can be considered your profit, the profit you earned by doing the assembly. Nobody paid you for it, but that's what you saved by doing it, so it represents real money in your pocket. That's the value you created. You didn't take the $700 from anyone. No one had to write you a check (and as an added benefit, you don't have to pay any income tax on it). What you did was take an undelivered, unassembled desk worth approximately $800 and you delivered it and assembled it so that it became the equivalent of something you would have gladly paid $1500 for.

Profit is nothing more than the value that is added by virtue of things such as effort, creativity, originality, convenience, and expertise. Profit does not represent stealing or taking. Profit represents giving and creating, building and nurturing, and making things more valuable.

Yes, but what about corporate profits? What about when a large oil company makes tens of billions of dollars and the price of gasoline is so high that ordinary people can barely afford to buy it? Well, that oil company has invested enormous amounts of money in developing the capabilities to find the oil under the ground and under the sea, extract it, transport it, refine it and distribute it as gasoline to consumers. If the company did not make a profit, it would not be able to continue doing all those things. There would be no incentive. No one would invest the money to create a company that could not make a profit.

Plus, the oil company has competitors who do the same things. If any company starts charging too much for their products, that represents an opportunity for their competitors to take business away by selling similar products for lower prices. Have you ever noticed how one gas station will lower its price and then the station across the street will respond by lowering its price? That's the free market. That's the value of competition. It's a mechanism that rewards the most efficient value producers. Corporate profits, just like any other profits, represent value added. As massive as they can sometimes appear, they are really very reasonable because they are constantly subject to the brutally disciplined forces of the marketplace (which is, by the way, a much more authentic expression of true democracy than any government anywhere on earth, because people get to vote every day with every purchase). When you hear that a large, successful corporation has made a large profit, that's cause to celebrate. Because what it means is that the corporation has injected a large amount of value into the world, value that was not there before, value that most likely benefits you and those around you in many different ways. Corporate profits, like all other profits, do not take anything away from life. They represent value added to life.

Dreams are what push people to create that value. The power of a billion dreams is a power that is unleashed by human freedom and a power that is fulfilled through individual human responsibility. It is not a power that must be forced on anyone. Rather, it harnesses natural self-interest in a positive and beneficial way. It is a power that can simply and easily be allowed. It is the power that transformed The United States of America from a small, young, poor country into the richest, most powerful nation the world has ever known. The power of a billion dreams creates innovation and industry and progress and products and wealth from little more than sheer desire.

Over time, the power of dreams naturally makes people and organizations more efficient, effective, accountable and creative. And it does this all without any centralized planning, and without forcing people to do things against their will.

As we have seen, life can be very unfair. At the same time, life has the possibility of being beautiful, rich and fulfilling. The power of a billion dreams arises to bridge the gap, creating great beauty and richness for more and more people in spite of life's inherent difficulty and unfairness.

From authentic dreams, meaningful value is created. When one person dreams, and follows that dream, one life is immensely enriched and that richness spills over into other lives. When a whole group of people are free to dream, and to follow their dreams, history is made. When the entire world dreams its ten billion unique, individual dreams, it's impossible to imagine the extent of the great richness that can result, yet it's clear to see that it will indeed be outstanding.

The Power of Ten Billion Dreams

Your Authentic Dreams

The thing that is really hard, and really amazing,
is giving up on being perfect and beginning the work of
becoming yourself.

— Anna Quindlen

We've seen how beneficial dreams can be for the whole world. Now it's time to get personal. Your dreams are good for the world, and your dreams are good for you, too. In fact, they're the very definition of what's good in your life. If you're alive, you have to be dreaming, and following those dreams. That's how you fulfill your beautiful and unique purpose.

So, how do you feel right now? Do you feel completely and totally fulfilled? Of course not. Even the most highly accomplished people never feel completely fulfilled, and that's a good thing. It means there's always something more, something meaningful, left to do. There's always a new way to experience even more fulfillment.

Fulfillment is not about getting filled up. When your car runs low on gas, you stop at a gas station and fill the tank. There's only so much you can put in the tank. After that, if you put in any more, it overflows. Yet as soon as you drive away from the gas pump, the tank begins to empty. It will only hold so much fuel at one time, but even if it is filled to the limit, soon there will be room for more.

Just as your gas tank will never be permanently filled, your life will never be totally fulfilled. As good as it gets, it can get even better. As far as you've already journeyed, you can fill up the tank again and experience even more.

Exactly how do you feel right now? What things in your life are you most thankful for? What things in your life could use some improvement? How do you feel about all that?

What you're feeling, whenever you feel anything, is your purpose. Sometimes it's a painful or uncomfortable feeling, when your outer life is not in harmony with your inner purpose. Other times it is a joyful feeling, when you are doing things that resonate well with your purpose. Yet no matter what you feel, or how it feels, or how intensely you feel it, what you are feeling is some manifestation of your purpose.

Real, authentic dreams connect directly to that purpose. A dream that you have for your life is actually an intention to express your own unique purpose in some specific way. The only dreams you can ever really fulfill are the authentic ones, and they're the ones that are based on your purpose. The most important step in achieving a dream is in choosing one that's real and meaningful and significant for you.

That would seem to be easy, yet it can be very difficult. What makes it so difficult? There's a lot of noise out there—things that sound like dreams, but really aren't. The way to cut through the noise is by asking why, and by challenging yourself to come up with an answer. It's going to take more than one answer, though. When you have the first answer, you must ask why again, and again. In fact, you must continue asking why until you get to an answer that is the essence of who and what you are.

This kind of inquiry is difficult, because it brings you face to face with yourself. Not that that's such a bad thing—it's most certainly a very good thing. It's just extremely intense, seeking to know yourself. Once you get there, though, you'll discover immense power for creating outstanding and meaningful value. That, of course, is what dreams are all about.

Here come's the hard part.

Answer this question: What do you really want?

If you said you want a BMW 335i with a Deep Sea Blue exterior and a Beige Dakota Leather interior, sorry, that's not good enough. Yes, I'd like one of those too, but the question is not "what stuff do you want?" The question is, "what do you really want?"

Let's try it again.

What do you really want?

Like I said, this is the hard part. And it's really, really hard. It's also really, really necessary. You can't skip it. Nothing else works unless you work this out.

The BMW, or the private island, or the sailing trip to Barbados, or the school you want to build for children in

Africa—those things are all great, but they're not what you really want. They're merely ways to take you to what you really want.

What you really want is not something you can possess. What you really want is not even something you can experience. What you really want it not a relationship of any kind.

What you really want is to feel a certain way.

So, how do you want to feel?

You don't really want that BMW, and as soon as you accept that, you're well on your way to having it. You don't really want to write a best-selling novel, and as soon as you accept that, you can actually begin to do it.

Does that sound crazy?

For anything you can imagine to desire, for any dream you can dare to dream, the possibility is already within you. In fact, you don't want anything, not really. Because in a very real and meaningful way, you already have it all. It's all yours. You simply must accept it and live it by letting it unfold in your life. It's all there for you to claim. But it's not what you want. Thinking that you want something merely drives it away from you.

Why is it so hard to figure out what you, really, truly, authentically want? Because there is nothing you really, truly, authentically want. Instead of figuring out what you want, figure out who you are. Then, come up with some meaningful and creative and compelling ways to express that.

There's nothing you want because you already have it all within the realm of your possibilities. You really, truly have it all. After all, you're alive in a universe of expanding abundance. Any thought of lack or limitation is a lie, based in fear, that keeps you from acknowledging and manifesting your dreams. It's very likely that you fear your awesome power. Why would you fear that power? Because it exposes who you truly are.

There is one thing most people fear more than death. It is public speaking. Public speaking exposes who you truly are. You may be able to hide most of yourself when you're in a one-on-one conversation, or interacting in a small group. But when you're up in front of a large group of people, and they all have their attention focused on you, you're frighteningly outnumbered. You can't maintain the illusion. They can see right through you, it seems, it feels. A thousand eyes are watching you. They can see all the way into your innermost recesses. If you're like most people, you're profoundly afraid of exposing who you truly are. What is that? Why is that?

Why are you so afraid of who you are? More specifically, why are you so reluctant to admit and express the beauty of who you are? Because who you are is all you have. If you expose it and it somehow falls short, then you have nothing. If you put it out there and somebody somehow takes it away from you, then you fall into oblivion, never to return, never to matter again.

But the thing is, that won't happen. It cannot happen. There is nothing to fear. The fear is a lie. The fear is a deception. As long as you have the courage to act, you will matter. Your actions in any given moment may fall pathetically short of the goal. You may in fact pick yourself up and make another attempt, giving the entirety of your focus and energy to it, and that second attempt could fall short as well. Even so, you matter. You matter very much. You are unique and beautiful in your very own way and always able to take the next step and to make some kind of a difference, to have some kind of an influence.

If you're even the slightest bit ambitious, it's going to take a while to fulfill that ambition, to fully express your dream. It will take multiple attempts. It will demand much of you. Don't punish or disrespect yourself for that. Just keep going. You have something important and meaningful to do, so keep going until you get it done. Then set your sights on an even more ambitious goal and quickly begin moving confidently toward it.

What you fear, ultimately, is your own success at being you. But that, it turns out, is nothing to fear. Your greatest fulfillment is in being you.

The most difficult part of fully manifesting your dream is knowing and acknowledging what it is. Once you know, once you're absolutely positive, then it's mostly a matter of going through the motions until you're there. In fact, once you know, once you take the first step on the path, you're suddenly living the dream.

The Power of Ten Billion Dreams

Imagine that! If you're clear and authentic about what your dream is, you can really, truly be living that dream in the next five minutes. No, it won't be fully manifested; you wouldn't want it to be. Yet from the moment you take the first step, you'll be living your dream.

Sure, there will be challenges along the way. Yet the biggest challenge by far is making a particular, specific commitment as to exactly what that way will be.

Why is it so difficult? Because to really, truly connect with your authentic dream, you have to fully and completely open yourself up and express who you truly are. That can be terrifying. It leaves you with no place to hide, and it also is very beautiful. Because who you are, is truly amazing.

If you have a constant, gnawing feeling that something is missing in your life, then ask yourself this. What do you really, truly desire to do with your life, right now?

With anything you sincerely care about, there are two possibilities. Either you want it, or you have it. Those possibilities are mutually exclusive. When you have it, you do not want it, because it is already yours. When you want it, you do not have it. Living your dream is a matter of letting go of the want, and allowing the having. The having begins immediately, and grows with each positive, purposeful action you take.

When you want something, you're focused primarily on the fact that you don't have it. The ironic thing is, you could easily begin to have it if you would just let go of the want.

That truth was made powerfully clear to me several years ago when we purchased the house where we now live. With the help of a real estate agent, we had been seriously looking for a house for a couple of months, and had even made a few offers, none of which had resulted in a contract.

Then one evening I was looking at listings on the web, and saw one that had not been there earlier in the day. The house had just been put up for sale that day and it looked like it exactly met all of our requirements. Although it was already dark outside, the whole family jumped in the car and drove over to the address. On the way over, we excitedly called our real estate agent and asked her to arrange a showing as soon as possible. Though we couldn't see much that evening in the dark, what we could see looked great.

Our agent arranged a showing the next morning. The house was indeed perfect. It had everything we were looking for. Plus it had a huge backyard with a natural wooded area that was like a private little national forest, along with a pool and beautiful landscaping. The only catch was this. The sellers were asking a good bit more than we thought the house was worth. We had looked at dozens of homes in the preceding couple of months and were very much in tune with the local market. The owners of this particular house lived out of state, so we knew that we had a better feel for the local market than they did.

As soon as we finished the showing, we instructed our agent to make an offer on the house. The next day, the sellers made a counter offer, which we still thought was too high. We went back to the house, measured the rooms to get an idea of exactly how our furniture would fit, and responded to their counter offer with a counter offer of our own, a little higher than our original offer.

After another day, the sellers responded with yet another offer, and said it would be their final offer. Although it was within just a few thousand dollars of our most recent offer, we still felt it was too high, and that the house would not appraise for that amount. Though we were already pre-qualified for financing that would have covered the sellers' final offer, we declined the offer and did not make any further offers of our own.

It was an extremely difficult decision. Here was the perfect house, meeting all our requirements, and we were letting it go. I was particularly enamored with the back yard, and had excitedly downloaded satellite photographs of the property and the adjoining greenbelt with its trails through a wooded hill country canyon. I really, really wanted that house and that property. But we were not going to pay more than what we knew it was worth. I clearly remember the moment I made the conscious decision to fully and completely let it go. It was not meant to be, I concluded. And I intentionally let go of an enormous amount of wanting. Yes, I felt disappointed. And yet I also felt empowered.

I'll never forget the next morning, getting the call. It was a Saturday in early April. We were preparing to go to the opening day festivities at the Little League park where our daughters played softball. Our agent called with the news that the sellers had reconsidered. They had accepted our previous offer! She was faxing the contract to us.

Later, over at the ballpark, while helping with the opening day activities, the realization hit me. As soon as I had completely let go of the wanting to get that house, I got it. It was a powerful lesson that has served me well in many other situations in the years since. We closed on the house a few weeks later and have loved living here ever since.

Stop looking at your dream as something you want. The moment you do that, it begins to become real. Let go of the want. Focus on gratitude for the infinite possibilities available to you. And focus on the why. Focus on the love. Focus on your purpose.

I dream of sailing from Corpus Christi, Texas to Barbados.

Why?

I love the ocean and I love to sail.

Why?

The ocean connects my spirit to the energy of limitless abundance. Sailing my own boat across the ocean gives me a way to tap into that limitless abundance and fulfill specific possibilities.

That sounds like too much mumbo jumbo. Let's give it another shot. Why do I love the ocean?

It inspires me.

Why does the ocean inspire me?

I feel a sense of awe when I am there.

Why do I feel a sense of awe, and why is that important to me?

From the ocean, I can experience the raw energy of creation. In the wind that fills my boat's sails, I feel that same energy in a different form. Feeling that energy gives me a profound and overwhelming appreciation for the miracle that is my existence, and the miracle that is all of creation.

Why?

Knowing that I am alive and aware, and that there are

limitless possibilities on top of limitless possibilities, fills my entire being with joy.

Why?

I live for possibilities, and to fulfill the most beautiful possibilities.

Why?

Because that is who I am. That is simply and fundamentally who I am.

Now it's your turn. What do you dream of, and why? Answer that question, and then ask why again. Be honest. Be relentless. Keep asking why. Keep answering honestly. This is your beautiful and unique life and your treasured dream we're talking about. Keep asking why until you connect with your very essence. Keep asking why, and lead yourself to a wonderful and authentic dream for your life that is uniquely yours. With that dream, you will absolutely change the world.

The Power of Ten Billion Dreams

Passion

*The more intensely we feel about an idea or a goal, the more
assuredly the idea, buried deep in our subconscious, will direct
us along the path to its fulfillment.*

— Earl Nightingale

Here's another thing to consider when zeroing in on your
dream: passion.

Passion is what enables you to live your dream. Passion
can take something you're interested in, something you'd like
to do, something that seems like it would be nice, and turn it
into reality. Passion takes your dream and brings it to life.

You can have all the skills. You can have all the resources.
You can have all the time, You can have all the knowledge and
all sorts of great connections. Yet if you don't have passion,
nothing is going to happen with all that stuff.

Or, you can have nothing. You can have not a cent to your
name. You can have no knowledge of how you're going to do
what you intend to do. You can have no connections with anybody, and you can be limited in the time available. And yet, if
you've got passion, then you'll find a way. You'll find a way to
get the resources. You'll find a way to meet the right people.
Your passion will connect you with them. Your passion will
connect you with the energy and the time and the money and
whatever else you require to get the job done.

The passion, if it's authentic—and that's the only kind
of passion there really is—your passion will connect you to
whatever it is you require. You can't be truly passionate about
something you don't care about. By very definition it's impossible. You cannot be passionate unless it means something to
you.

That's why it's so important to land on a dream that means
something to you, a dream that is truly yours, not one that's
borrowed, not an imitation, but something that's you. It must
be something that when you think about it makes you feel
right, makes you feel that yes, this is the way life is intended

to be, this is the way I am supposed to be, this is what I was born to experience. That's why it's so crucial to challenge your dream by asking why, and by continuing to ask why until there is no answer other than because it's just the way you are.

You were born to see the world in a certain way, to experience the world in a certain way, to feel things that no one else has ever felt. Living your dream is how you will do it. The passion for reaching that experience, for making that dream come to life, is where the energy comes from. That's the raw material for achievement—the passion of a dream.

What is it you dream about? What is it you care about? What is it that makes you frustrated? What is it that makes you angry? What is it that makes you filled with joy, filled with pride, filled with a sense that all is right with the world? What is it that you consider to be beautiful? What kinds of situations do you seek out? What would you do if you had all the money in the world, all the time in the world, all the resources in the world, all the abilities and knowledge and wisdom in the world? What would you do with it all? How would you put it to use in a way that was what you really felt great about doing? Ask yourself that. What would you do? And whatever that is, no matter whether it's practical or reasonable or politically correct or compassionate, or courteous, or not, whatever that is, that's what you must be doing.

That's what will fulfill you. That's what will make the most of the beautiful potential of your life. That is what will enable you to make your highest and best contribution to life. That's what will enable you to create a legacy that is unlike any other, with great value that continues on and on without end.

You can do it. It's within you to do it. It's what you are here for, to do it. So think. And don't just think, but feel. Feel how you feel and examine those feelings. Question those feelings. Challenge those feelings. Ask where they come from. Ask, what is it that makes them arise within you? Find the passion.

Think of a time when you felt better than you've ever felt in your whole life. What were you doing and why? What made you feel that way?

You choose every feeling that you experience. So, on that particular occasion, in that particular circumstance, in that particular time, why did you choose that feeling, that wonderful feeling that felt better than anything you've ever experienced. Why did you choose to feel that way? What was it that gave rise to that feeling? That's what you want to understand, because that's what you want to create more of. That's what you want to expand upon.

You want to take that feeling that's the most wonderful feeling you've ever felt and make it into a valley instead of a peak. Go even higher. Go so high that that most wonderful feeling you've ever felt, looks almost trivial by comparison. Because you can, and you must. That's what you're here for—to live, fully.

You're here to fulfill your own unique values, your own unique perspective, your own unique view of life. Your uniqueness is the most valuable thing you have. Otherwise, why would you even be here? If you were the same as everybody else, what purpose would it be for you to live your life? But the thing is, you're not. You're definitely not the same as anyone else.

Your life has a very clear and definite purpose, and you can feel that purpose in the authentic joy you experience. You can even feel that purpose in the despair you experience. You can feel that purpose in the good times and the bad times, and in the way you relate to whatever is going on. You can feel that unique purpose that is you. What is it? Challenge yourself to find it. It's not easy to find what it is.

Emotionally, it can be the hardest thing you've ever done. Because it's scary. It's scary to confront your true essence. It's scary to realize there's only one of you. In all time and all eternity, there's only one of you. In the whole universe, there's only one of you. That's an awesome and a dreadful responsibility. But it's beautiful, too. It is the definition of beauty itself. It is the way that beauty can know itself, through you, through your own unique perspective. That's how beauty becomes beautiful.

Yes, find your passion. But don't stop at merely finding your passion. Immerse yourself in that passion. Day in and day out, in everything you do and everything you say, in the thoughts you think and the feelings you have, live the passion.

Let it fill you with energy. Let it fill you with great ideas. Let it fill you with determination to fulfill all the best possibilities. Let passion fill your life, and your life will be full indeed. It will be full of the things that really mean something to you.

Passion. Find it, live it, and bring your dreams to life.

The Ocean

We are tied to the ocean. And when we go back to the sea, whether it is to sail or to watch—we are going back from whence we came.

— John F. Kennedy

    The first place I ever sailed a boat on the ocean was at Corpus Christi. Well, technically it was the ocean, though it was an extremely protected little patch of water. I was 13 years old. Our family had trailered our fun little 13-foot red and white fiberglass sloop from the suburbs of Dallas to Corpus for spring break. This particular sailing adventure was not in the open waters of the Gulf of Mexico. It was really not even in Corpus Christi Bay. We launched the boat in the harbor and never got outside the breakwater. Still, the wind was good, a beautiful memory was made, and a dream began to take shape.

    Before that trip, I had only sailed on inland lakes. I was beginning to be captivated by sailing, though. The small boat we sailed on a few Dallas-area lakes was a lot of fun. When it was not in the water, it sat in our garage. The boat was too small to have a cabin, but there was a covered compartment where the sails were stored that was just big enough for a 13-year-old kid to climb inside and dream of crossing the ocean. That's exactly what I dreamed about, urged on by stories in *National Geographic* about the adventures of Robin Lee Graham, who set out at age 16 and eventually sailed all the way around the world in a 24-foot sloop.

    After a few years my parents traded up to a 22-foot sailboat that did have a small cabin, which they kept berthed at a local marina. With that boat came the experience of spending the night at anchor and falling asleep to the sound of waves lapping against the hull. That further intensified my love of being on the water.

    Not only did I fall in love being out on the water, I also

realized how much I loved being near the ocean. Though I have never lived on the coast, for most of my life I've lived within a few hours' drive of the ocean. And through the years, I've never gone for very long without a visit to the seashore. Many of those visits have been to Corpus Christi, which is about a four and a half hour drive from Austin, where I've lived for the last 30 years. Before Austin, I lived for a couple of years in Houston, which is very much a coastal city. One of my friends had a bay house on Galveston Island. From my apartment in southwest Houston, I could be there in about an hour. The parties would start on Friday night and continue until Sunday afternoon. In my early twenties I took a breath of the damp, salty air and ever since then I've always wanted more.

It was also during those years in Houston that I began my journeys to the islands of the Caribbean Sea, though it would be nearly three decades before I ever made it to Barbados. I found another love while living in Houston my wife, Karen. By the time we got married I had moved to Austin and had bought my own boat, a 23-foot sloop berthed on Lake Travis. Karen and I honeymooned on the beautiful Caribbean island of Saint Martin, where I had the opportunity to take the helm of a sailboat in the real ocean.

The ocean is as close to eternity as anything I can touch. True, I can look up at the stars on a clear night and see back to a time before there ever was an ocean. Yet in the daylight, in the tactile realm, the ocean is the most nearly eternal thing I can behold. Though the stars are all distant, and many even more distant, the ocean is here in front of me, and distant at the same time. I can feel its expanse as I stand on its edge, though I know what I see is only a tiny fraction. And the ocean is unceasingly restless. Its waves crash endlessly upon the shore, as far up and down the coast as I can see. It can carry me all the way around the globe if I have the courage to undertake such a journey. It can also swallow me up in an instant. I feel the intoxicating mixture of awe and dread, and I cannot stay away from it. I make no apologies for my addiction, but give in to it as often as I can.

The Power of Ten Billion Dreams

Think of how very much energy it takes just to shove one wave upon the shore. The ocean does it every few seconds on every stretch of coastline all over the planet. Early on New Year's Day in 2008, I sat alone in a hot-water spa on the deck of a massive cruise ship. There had been a big party the night before to welcome in the new year, with champagne being uncorked, poured and consumed by the case. All the other passengers were sleeping it off, providing me with solitude to contemplate the rising sun. We were in the Pacific Ocean, far enough off the coast of Mexico that no land was visible. Only water in every direction. The ocean, the biggest one there is.

As I sat in the warm water of the hot tub, I could see the horizon. And I noticed it was very slowly, and yet very steadily rocking. Of course it was the ship that was rocking, not the horizon. Yet we were in calm waters. It was not the motion of ordinary waves making the horizon appear to rock. The slow and steady rocking, taking a full minute or so to complete each cycle, was coming from massive swells. As the ship rode up and down those swells it would rock just a few degrees back and then a few degrees forward, so little as to be unnoticeable if one wasn't keeping an eye on the horizon. The swells were not high, but they were very long.

On that bright, clear New Year's morning I watched the horizon slowly and repeatedly tilt one way and then the other. I pushed the button to turn off the air-bubble jets in the hot tub. As the water I was sitting in became calm, it too began to rock back and forth, slowly and steadily, in time with the horizon. I've been on many a rocking boat before, but had never experienced such a long cycle. How long and how far, I wondered, had these swells been traveling?

What I then realized was that I was observing something akin to the very pulse of the planet itself. In that moment I could feel my surroundings on a cosmic scale. It's not often that we can literally sense being on the surface of a massive sphere that floats in space and orbits around an even more massive star. Yet on that day, in that spot, riding those steady ocean swells, that's exactly what I experienced. Time stood still and eternity stretched in all directions. This was not some manufactured, special-effect thrill ride arranged by the cruise line. The swells had been heaving their way through this stretch of ocean since long before recorded history, and will continue to do so long after anyone is around to notice them.

That's the kind of experience one can have on the ocean. For me, it makes me feel wonderfully alive, and that's what I'm here to do.

Allowing Your Dreams

Every great dream begins with a dreamer. Always remember, you have within you the strength, the patience, and the passion to reach for the stars to change the world.

— Harriet Tubman

It starts as a fragile, wispy thing that might float right on by unnoticed. Except, it snags on something within your soul and lodges there. And then you start to feel it. Yes, it feels good. But it also hurts. It aches, because you desperately long to bring it to life.

So, caught in between that wonderful vision of what can be, and that painful realization of what has not yet been fulfilled, you know you've got to do something about it. And your passion begins to build. And that makes you want it even more. It begins to gnaw at you, urging you constantly to do something, do something, do something about it.

With a determination that you just can't deny, you take the first step. And it feels good. It feels powerful. And though you don't even know what the next step will be, you resolve to figure it out, and you do, and you take that next step, and the next. Driven forward by pure, raw desire, you refuse to listen to those who tell you it can't be done.

And though you get knocked around relentlessly, still you find a way, a way to get back up and run, ride, walk or crawl forward, whatever it takes, every time. Because it's your dream. It's your purpose. It's what you're here to do. It's your gift to give to all that is. You know, beyond knowing, that you must.

With a power you feel in every fiber of your being, but cannot fully explain, you bring the dream to life. And the joy of fulfillment is more intense than you ever could have imagined.

To live, you must dream. To dream, you must live.

It is a beautiful cycle, and a powerful one. Dreams push life forward, and not only for those who dream them. One person's dream can benefit the whole world. Even in just one dream, there is that much power. Dreams energize life, and give that energy a specific and valuable direction. And life, in turn, inspires and enables more dreams.

The fulfillment in your life comes from following your dreams. And from the fulfillment you've already created will come new, even more meaningful dreams. From one dream to the next, your life proceeds. And it is in the living toward those dreams that you experience the beautiful substance of your existence.

Within you is a dream that is always there, and from that dream comes the possibility of every other dream. Every time you feel joy, you feel that dream. Every time you feel sadness, you feel that dream. In fact, every time you feel anything, you feel that dream. Because even though your dream is uniquely yours, in one way it is like every dream that every person has ever had. Your dream is all about how you would like for life to be. When you see life as being in harmony with your dream, even if it is only a little glimpse, you allow yourself to feel joy. When you sense that life is not going the way you imagine to be best, you feel sadness, or one of many other negative emotions.

What do you often worry about? Whatever it is, imagine that it is no longer possible and can never be. Imagine that you are completely and forever free of your worry and of the object of that worry. That freedom is what your deepest dream feels like. You may not be able to express it in words, yet you know the feeling.

Your most fundamental dream, the dream from which all your other dreams spring, is, at its heart, the feeling that life is good, and right, peaceful and meaningful. It is the feeling you feel when you know life is at its best. From that one defining and immutable dream come your likes and dislikes, your interests and passions, your opinions, and the values you treasure. At your heart, you are that dream. For the substance of that fundamental dream is a dream to be the unique person you are. And from that dream will come many other dreams that nourish and support and express it.

As such, it is impossible to logically analyze or objectively understand your most fundamental dream, that dream from which all others are born. For it is you. It is your essence. It

The Power of Ten Billion Dreams

is your purpose. You can think about it, and feel about it, and talk with other people about it. Yet you must always do so from a biased perspective. For when you speak of your defining dream, what you are talking about, is what is doing the talking. Though you cannot fully understand your dream in an intellectual way, you can know it, more and more fully each day. Indeed, that is the story of your life, to live out the dream that is you.

And from that one dream, many other dreams will continue to come. Those dreams will indeed be very specific and rich with detail. Those are the dreams you can act upon. Those are the dreams with which you can give your own unique value to the world. Those are the dreams that will compel you to learn, to love, to think, to act, to persist and then to give birth to even more dreams. Your dreams connect who you are on the inside with what you can accomplish in the world. Because of that, every one of those dreams has great power, not only for you, but for all of life.

So what are those dreams? Where do you find them? How do you create them? How do you know they are real? How do you know they are authentically yours?

The way to know and to formulate your dreams is simple. Pay attention to life and to the way you feel about it, be honest with yourself, and the dreams will come. Powerful, purposeful, meaningful dreams will come. It's very simple, yet it can also be very difficult.

Giving birth to a dream is not an intellectual exercise. Certainly it's true that fleshing out your dream, and working to achieve that dream, will definitely require the use of your intelligence. But having the dream in the first place, that comes from somewhere deeper. It comes from the way you feel, but not just from any feelings.

What are your feelings, anyway? Think back on the feelings you've had throughout your life. One thing that's easy to see is that you experience feelings on several different levels. There are the physical feelings of your body. You feel warmth, you feel pain, you feel hungry, you feel tired, and you experience all sorts of other feelings related to your physical existence. Then there are intellectual feelings such as opinions and ideas. You feel that certain things are true and certain other things are not true, based on the facts you're aware of and the experiences you've had, and the way you interpret those things in your mind. Still other feelings are ego-driven emotional feelings. These include feelings such as sadness, optimism, lust, comfort, resentment and confidence. And finally there are the feelings of your spirit such as joy, peace, faith and knowing. These feelings of your spirit are feelings that have no doubt or judgment attached to them. They go beyond ideas and logical constructions. They are pure feelings that you experience as undeniable truth at the very core of your being.

Those feelings of your spirit are what will resonate with your authentic dreams. When you pay attention to life, and to the way you feel about what you see, those deepest feelings of your spirit are the ones to listen to. Have you ever gone some place that you've never been before and immediately felt at home there? That's the kind of feeling we're talking about here. From such a feeling, your most powerful and authentic dreams can grow. Have you ever met a person and immediately had the feeling that you've known that person all your life? Have you ever done something for the first time and had the feeling that it's something you were always meant to do? Feelings such as these will point you toward creating dreams that bring great value not only in your own life, but also in the lives of many others.

Pay attention to those feelings, and to life, and ask yourself why. Why does a certain film, or book, or person, or place inspire you? What is it within you, what value, what desire, what longing is it that resonates with life's beauty and wonder? Questions such as these are not questions to be answered directly. The important thing is to ask them, with sincerity, and with the expectation that the answers will come not in words, but in the form of heightened awareness. Notice what you feel, ask yourself why, and you'll open yourself for allowing new dreams to take shape.

You cannot create a meaningful, authentic dream through sheer determination. But then, you don't really need to. Your dreams come when you simply allow them.

Once you connect with an authentic dream, a dream that is

truly an expression of who you are and of how you genuinely desire to be, the positive power of that dream begins to flow into every corner of your world. Fully bringing that dream into reality will take time and effort, and that is good. That's where the real value of your dream shines through. Making your dream come true is a process, but it's not necessarily a process that you can plan out in advance. Rather, just as with creating the dream in the first place, it is a matter of allowing.

To live your dream, keep that dream at the forefront of your awareness. Look at the world and look at your life from the perspective of your dream. When challenges appear in your life, look at them from the perspective of your dream. When opportunities become available to you, look at those opportunities from the perspective of your dream. Your authentic dream will enable you to see what to do. Just as importantly, that dream will constantly remind you why you're doing what you do. Stay connected to your dream and you will be persistent in your efforts. You will have no problem finding the discipline necessary to undertake complicated, demanding tasks. You will find a way to find the skills and resources and connections that you must find.

Life can indeed be very difficult when you follow your dreams. Life is much more difficult, though, when you turn your back on your dreams. The difficulties you encounter in following your dreams are difficulties that can be overcome, difficulties that you have the ability to transcend, and difficulties that your dream will enable you to push your way through. In contrast, the difficulties you encounter if you abandon your dreams will never go away. Those difficulties cannot be transcended.

You must summon great amounts of courage, commitment and faith in order to create meaningful dreams in the first place and then to follow those dreams. And though the work is difficult, it also has its own unique beauty. In doing the work of following your dreams, you lay claim to the great value of those dreams. In the achieving of your dreams you find the realization of those dreams. And in allowing your dreams to come to life, you give your own beautiful and unique gifts to all that is.

The Power of Ten Billion Dreams

Dealing With Doubt

Doubts and mistrust are the mere panic of timid imagination, which the steadfast heart will conquer, and the large mind transcend.

— Helen Keller

Ultimately, the only thing that can completely kill your dream is your own doubt. Your dream can survive every other challenge, and even thrive on them. But if you begin to doubt your dream, and then allow that doubt to grow, there will soon be nothing left of your dream.

Doubt is insidious. You feel it, and you know instinctively it's there to steal your dream, so your natural inclination is to fight it. Yet that just makes your doubt stronger. Fighting your doubt gives it more legitimacy, and that's the last thing you want.

Doubts can be sparked by the tiniest little things. Even an occurrence that would otherwise be positive can give rise to doubt. Imagine that your dream is to live in a home that's high up in the mountains. You know you absolutely love being in the mountains during all seasons of the year, and you are working each day toward your dream. Then you happen to go for a week to visit a friend who lives in a beautiful home on the beach. The whole experience is very enjoyable. As a result you start to wonder whether or not you really want to live in the mountains. After all, living on the beach is nice, too. Suddenly, a seed of doubt is planted in your mind. It's not the result of anything negative. On the contrary, it was your positive experience at the beach that gave rise to the doubt. Very soon, though, the doubt can indeed become negative. If left unchecked it can lay waste to your dream. Now it may very well be that you would enjoy living at the beach even more than living in the mountains. If that's the case, then you can certainly modify your dream. But it's just as likely that, although your time at the beach was a lot of fun, and it was a great place to visit, you wouldn't really want to live there permanently. The point here is to show that even positive experiences can cause doubts to arise.

Of course, negative thoughts and experiences can also bring doubt into your life. One of the most common kinds of doubt is doubt in your very ability to reach your dream. That's a tough one, because it's a doubt that increasingly reinforces its own premise. It's a doubt that usually begins when you experience some kind of setback, even a minor one. Instead of putting that setback in perspective, you are tempted to project that small setback far beyond its actual context, so it covers your entire dream in a cloak of impossibility. Instead of seeing the setback as one path that didn't take you where you thought it would, you can blow it all out of perspective and come to the conclusion that nothing you do will get you to the fulfillment of your dream. Does that sound familiar?

If you think you can't do something, you're absolutely right. The very thought of not being able to do it, prevents you from getting it done. Every action begins with a thought, and when the thought is that the action won't bring the result you want it to bring, that action is simply not going to happen.

Not only that, thinking you can't do something gives you a perfect excuse not to do it. After all, if you're not capable of reaching your dream then you are absolved from the responsibility of reaching it. In that case, your doubt actually becomes very comforting, which of course gives it even greater power and desirability.

In the long run, doubts make your life very difficult. However, in the short run, at any given moment, it's easier to doubt than it is to do. When you doubt that you can accomplish something, the doubt gives you a nice, comfortable place to hide, a reason for not making the effort. Yet if you keep piling up one doubt on top of another, soon there's no room left for your dream. When you seek refuge in the comfort of your doubts, you close yourself off from all the positive possibilities in your life. After a while even the comfort fades, as regret sets in. What was once very comfortable and reassuring turns into regret for opportunities missed that will never come again.

The most effective way to deal with doubt is to accept it, experience it, and then let it go. That process gives you complete control over your doubt, which is a much better strategy than letting doubt get control of you and all your thoughts. It also prevents you from giving power and increased legitimacy to the doubt by fighting against it.

Let's look for a moment at fighting against your doubt and see why it is such an undesirable option.

Have you ever had someone challenge some particular thing that you firmly believe? How did you respond to that person? Well, you probably came up with a long list of very valid reasons for why you believe what you believe. Now perhaps those reasons were sufficient to convince the other person of what you believe, or perhaps they weren't. Never mind the other person, though. What's certain is that, in expressing those reasons, you strengthened your own belief. The other person challenged you to prove your belief, you responded to the challenge, and your belief grew stronger as a result.

The same thing happens when you fight against your doubt. The only difference is, you're playing both roles, the believer and the skeptic. By fighting against your doubt, you challenge yourself (you are, after all, the originator and owner of that doubt) to prove the doubt. That begins an inner dialogue in which you argue for and against your doubt. No matter which side wins the argument, the doubt gets stronger. Because not only have you focused your thoughts on the doubt itself, you've also focused on a whole long list of reasons for maintaining that doubt, giving it increased presence and validity within your own thinking. Instead of getting rid of the doubt, you've enabled it to become more firmly entrenched. That might very well lead you to fight against it even more, escalating the whole process. Through it all, your doubt grows stronger and stronger.

So, if fighting against doubt doesn't get rid of it, what does?

I recently saw a really funny and fascinating YouTube video of a "trick play" that happened during a middle school football game. Both teams are lined up on the field, ready for the center to snap the ball to the quarterback. But instead of the quarterback taking the snap and aggressively passing, handing off, or running with the ball, fighting against the defensive players to gain yards, he simply taps the center on the shoulder. The center picks up the ball, turns around, and hands it to the quarterback. All the other offensive players remain lined up just where they are, and simply stand up in place, as if the referee has blown a whistle to stop the play. But there is no whistle. It's all a ruse. Meanwhile, the quarterback takes the ball from the center and walks calmly, slowly, and deliberately past the defensive linemen. The defensive players just stand there, not realizing that the ball is in play. Once the quarterback gets past most of the defensive linemen, he takes off running toward the goal line. By the time the other team realizes that the ball is actually in play, it's too late. The quarterback runs all the way to the goal line and scores an easy touchdown.

When I saw this video, I realized it was a great illustration of how to successfully deal with doubt. If the quarterback had snapped the ball in the usual way and tried to run down the field, the defensive players would have stopped him after just a few yards. He may not have even made it past the line of scrimmage. In the same way, if you aggressively fight against your doubt, your doubt will respond and fight back. You won't get very far. Instead, what the quarterback did was to fully accept and acknowledge the presence of the defensive players. Then he calmly and quite fearlessly experienced that defensive presence as he walked by the other team's players. Because he was so matter-of-fact in his stride, the defensive players didn't even attempt to stop him. In the same way, you can look calmly at your doubt and experience what it is saying, without challenging or fighting or arguing against that doubt, and without any fear. Finally, the quarterback in the video moved completely beyond the defensive players and took off running toward the goal line. In the same way, you can simply let go of your doubt and free yourself to move quickly in the direction of your dream.

Though your doubts can stop you, there's no reason to fear them. You can deal with every one of them. Whenever a doubt pops into your thinking, accept it. After all, the doubt is already there so you might as well acknowledge it. As soon as you do, you put yourself in control. Then, with no fear or apprehension, consider that doubt. Listen to it. Feel it. Focus on it. Wrap

The Power of Ten Billion Dreams

your attention around it. Choose to do these things, because when you're doing what you choose, you are in control. Then, exercising that same control, let go. Let go of that doubt. Let it fall quickly and cleanly away from you. Free yourself of it once and for all. Don't use up all your energy fighting against it and making it stronger. Simply free yourself to move beyond it and to move more quickly than ever before in the direction of your dreams.

Some time when you have a minute or two, try this exercise. Find some small object, such as a pencil or pen. Pick it up in one hand and acknowledge it. Look at it. Roll it around in your hand and realize that you have complete control over it. Realize also that you are choosing to hold it, to feel it, and to experience the reality of it. But it is not you. It is separate from you. It is something you are acknowledging. It is something that you've chosen to make a part of your experience, but it is not a permanent part of you. Then grasp it tightly, to the point where it becomes a little bit uncomfortable to do so. Finally, let it go. Let it fall quickly and effortlessly to the floor.

The next time you encounter a doubt, use the same strategy. Acknowledge it, allow it, examine it, focus on it and fully experience the reality of it, then just let it go. Just as with the pencil, the effort involved is in holding on to it. Letting go is nothing more than simply choosing to no longer hold on. It's really no effort at all, and it can get you quickly moving ahead. Practice it often, with every doubt. The quicker you can get through the process, the better.

What doubts have been holding you back? Doubt can seem very compelling, so much so that it feels like it's a part of you. But it is not. Doubt is nothing but a thought you have chosen to hold in your mind. Maybe there are things you can learn from it. Maybe there are some adjustments you can make to your dream because of it. Yet if you hold on to that doubt too long, it can kill your dream. Don't fear it, don't fight against it. Just see it for what it is, experience it, and let it go. Free yourself to move forward toward the achievement of your dream.

The Power of Ten Billion Dreams

Sailing to Anegada

*One doesn't discover new lands without consenting
to lose sight of the shore for a very long time.*
— Andre Gide

Many people ask me how I started *The Daily Motivator*. I usually tell about how I had always been interested in personal development, and that when the web came along I was fascinated the the possibilities it offered for providing daily positive reinforcement to people. That's all very true. Yet there was something else, a very meaningful event in my own life, that played a major role. It was an experience that opened up a window and allowed me to see inside to the glimmering reality of my dreams.

On a weekend afternoon in the fall of 1994, I received a phone call from my dear friend David Madden. David and his wife Cindy had been visiting with another couple, who are also great, life-long friends, Scott and Donna Broberg. The four of them had come up with the idea of a sailing trip in the Virgin Islands. Years prior to that, David, Cindy, Scott, Donna and Karen and I had all spent a delightful, memorable evening on my sailboat, on an inland lake near Austin. That night, we had dreamed about someday taking such a trip to the Virgin Islands. Now they were starting to make plans to actually do it.

Financially, and in other ways, it was not the best time for us. Our youngest daughter was only a year and a half old. In my graphics business, my best customer had recently cut back on the work they were giving me. The monthly rent for the office I was leasing had increased so much I could no longer afford it, so I had just finished moving my office to a room in our house. I had no idea where I would come up with the money for a sailing trip in the Virgin Islands, but I sure didn't want to miss out on it. So I told David to count us in, and the serious planning began. We booked a crewed charter out of Roadtown, Tortola on a 52-foot Beneteau sloop, *Ambience*. It would be the six of us, plus the captain and his wife, an accomplished chef trained at Le Cordon Bleu Paris, sailing around the British Virgin Islands for a week in June 1995.

Somehow we came up with the money for the charter and the airfare to Tortola. We arranged for Karen's parents to keep our younger, two-year-old daughter and for my parents to take care of our older daughter. A couple of months before the trip, my mother was diagnosed with breast cancer, underwent surgery, and was scheduled for chemotherapy that would begin while we were away on the sailing trip. Even so, she generously and selflessly insisted that we not change our plans, and said they would manage just fine with our daughter, who was seven at the time. Sixteen years later, as I write this, my mother is cancer free and doing very well.

In Austin that year, summer began early, as it very often does, and came on strong. About a week before we were scheduled to leave on the trip, the air conditioner in my car went out, making it almost unbearable to drive during the daytime. Normally, back in those days, I would have gotten all upset about something like that, worrying about the expense and inconvenience. But something was different that time. The dream of sailing through the Caribbean was close enough to touch. So I just filled up a plastic bag with ice to keep me cooled down while driving, put a smile on my face, and went about my errands in preparation for the trip.

The sailing trip was everything we hoped and dreamed it would be, and more. The combination of great friends, spectacular scenery, outstanding food, abundant fine wine, and exhilarating sailing combined to make it a trip of a lifetime. The most incredible part of an incredible week was our visit to the island of Anegada. True to its name, Anegada ("sunken" in Spanish) is the only island in the British Virgin Islands that is not mountainous. It is flat and low, formed from coral and limestone instead of being volcanic in origin like the other islands. Surrounding Anegada is a massive coral reef, one of the largest in the world. Anegada is a place apart, with miles of spectacular deserted beaches and great snorkeling.

We ended up spending two nights at Anegada instead of the one night we had planned to stay there. That gave us a whole day to spend just walking along the beach at Loblolly Bay and soaking up the immense tranquility of such a special place. Something about Anegada touched me deeply and re-connected me with some of my longest-held, authentic dreams. One of the most prominent of those dreams was to write. The next afternoon, with the sailboat moored at Marina Cay, that's exactly what I started to do. I pulled out a legal pad and pen, and begin to put my feelings and impressions on paper. It felt good and right, something I knew I was meant to do. Four months after we returned from that sailing trip, *The Daily Motivator* was born.

I had always had the dream to write, but for years I had merely been dancing around the edges of that dream. It was another dream, the dream of sailing in the Virgin Islands, that finally brought my dream of writing to the surface and compelled me to act on my dream of being a writer. It's a great example of how one dream can nourish another dream, and that dream can nourish many other dreams. When you dream, and follow that dream, you never know where that dream can take you. In my dream to sail in the Virgin Islands, I had no idea I would be led to the magical island of Anegada. I had no idea that it would inspire in me an insatiable desire to write about the goodness and beauty in this life. When you follow your dream, you cannot know all the places it will take you. Yet you can know for sure that where you go, will bring great fulfillment to the real, authentic person you are inside.

The Power of Ten Billion Dreams

Moving Past
the Setbacks

*You may not realize it when it happens, but a kick in the teeth
may be the best thing in the world for you.*
— Walt Disney

In the process of living your dream, you'll experience set-backs. Some of them will be due to your own mistakes and miscalculations. Others will be things that are completely out of your control, but which have a significant impact on what you seek to do.

Your authentic dream is your dream no matter what. The value of that dream is independent of whatever events and circumstances may come along. When a setback occurs, it can very often seem like your only option is to give up on your dream. But that's not the case at all. You are still you. Your deepest inner purposes and values are still yours. Your dream is still as meaningful as it always was. Just as importantly, your dream is still as possible and achievable is it has ever been.

When you're seeking to create any kind of significant and meaningful value, you absolutely will experience setbacks. In fact, the very value of the achievement itself is tied to the challenges, the obstacles and the setbacks that must be transcended. It may not seem so at the time you encounter them, but the setbacks can actually end up moving you more solidly in the direction of your dream.

In the spring and summer of 2001, my dream of being a successful, published writer was beginning to gain some real traction. I had already published my first book. Paid subscriptions to *The Daily Motivator* had begun to grow faster than ever, and website traffic was solid. I had been working on recording a three-hour audiocassette program, which was published in August of that year. The response to it was very good. Financially, my writing was bringing in enough money to pay the bills, but just barely. There was no money in the bank to cover a large unexpected expense. So of course that's exactly what happened.

On the first Thursday of September 2001 I was driving my fifteen-year-old Oldsmobile to to the bank, and stopped along the way to buy a cold drink. When I got back in the car and turned the key, the engine wouldn't start. It wasn't a just dead battery. It was much more serious than that. The old car was not worth what it would cost to repair it.

A bank where I had an account had recently sent me a notice that I was pre-qualified for a car loan, but it had to be on the purchase of a brand new car. I was accustomed to driving used cars and had never borrowed money to buy a vehicle, but at the time the loan offer from the bank looked like my best option. My business was on a good trajectory, the audio program was selling well, and I was confident that I'd easily be able to make the payments on a new car. So a few days after my car gave out, on Sunday afternoon, September 9, 2001, I drove home with a brand new minivan and a monthly car pay ment.

Less than two days later, the whole world changed. In the immediate aftermath of the September 11th terrorist attacks, people everywhere were in a state of shock. Not only were we grieving for the nearly unimaginable suffering and loss of life, no one knew what was coming next. Normal life was disrupted and put on hold in countless ways for weeks, and longer. Website traffic to *The Daily Motivator* was very high on the day after the attacks, but then it quickly dropped off. People were focused on other things. The traffic to the site slowed down considerably. The orders for subscriptions, books and my new audio program essentially dropped to zero. Existing subscribers even stopped renewing their subscriptions. Nobody knew what was coming next, and everyone just kind of froze in place.

Compared to the families with loved ones who had been killed or injured, my problems were indeed trivial. Still, they were very real. Suddenly, my ability to make the car payment, not to mention the ability to pay all the other bills, didn't look like such a sure thing. It was disconcerting to be sure, but just

The Power of Ten Billion Dreams

like everyone else, my attention was focused elsewhere. What would life be like now, for my family, in our community, in our country, in the world, I wondered? It was a time when I felt a kind of anxiety I had never felt before. It was a slow, gnawing anxiety. I knew I was not in immediate danger, but I also knew that many of the things I had taken for granted for my whole life were suddenly not so certain. I felt a disconcerting, vague fear, but I didn't know exactly what I was afraid of, and I certainly didn't know what to do about it. It was a helpless feeling.

Then I realized millions and millions of other people would almost certainly be feeling the same thing. Now that was the kind of problem I could do something about. I desperately wanted to give a positive gift to the world. I vowed to do something special that would bring some measure of encouragement and reassurance to people. I knew it needed to be something beautiful, peaceful and unique. That was when I came up with the "Right Now" presentation (if you're not familiar with it, go to www.PositivePause.com). Though I had never used that particular software program before, I purchased Macromedia Flash and taught myself the basics of how to make a "slide-show" type of animated web presentation, with text fading in and out of pictures. I found some stock photos of beautiful nature scenes, and as I contemplated each picture, the appropriate words came to me. Using Flash, I put it all together and published it on *The Daily Motivator* site. Then I sent an email to all *The Daily Motivator* subscribers letting them know about the presentation, and encouraging them to share it with others.

Yes, I was very concerned about the fact that my website traffic and orders had dropped off so severely. But that wasn't why I created the "Right Now" presentation. By that point I simply felt the desire to do something positive, something that would be my way of balancing out the extreme negativity that had invaded so many lives. I let go of all my concerns and reached deep within myself to find the most positive thing I could feel. The "Right Now" presentation is what came out. I published it on the website, then let it go. I really had no expectations. In fact, once the "Right Now" presentation was published, I didn't pay much attention to it. I moved on to other things.

Yet within a few months, that little five-minute presentation would change everything.

In December 2001, a few days before Christmas, I started looking at the web traffic and sales numbers, and realized that they were higher than they had ever been. Not only that, the numbers seemed to be quickly growing on a daily basis. Within a couple of weeks after that, the growth became explosive. Hundreds of people each day were purchasing subscriptions.

What happened? Where was it all coming from?

The "Right Now" presentation I had created back in September had gone viral. Its peaceful message was resonating with thousands and thousands of people, and many of the people who viewed it would quickly recommend it to their friends. It was putting *The Daily Motivator* on the map. My dream of making a positive difference in the world through writing was coming true before my eyes.

Soon I was working harder and more intensely than I had ever worked in my life. I had a tiger by the tail. The slide show format of the Right Now presentation was responsible for bringing in thousands of new subscribers, and those new subscribers were wanting to see the daily messages in a similar format. Previously the daily messages had been available only as text, yet because of the overwhelming demand I worked out the programming so that they could also be available in with the words fading in and out of beautiful nature photos, just like the Right Now presentation. It was a very hectic time, and yet also a very exciting time.

What had been an immense setback to my dream had compelled me to dig deeper, to find a message that was more authentic than anything I had written before, and to present that message in a new, creative and powerful way. As horrible and tragic as the events of September 2001 were, they had awakened in many people a new sense of positive meaning and purpose. That was certainly the case with me, and I was in a position to express that positive meaning though *The Daily Motivator* website and the "Right Now" presentation.

The positive value I expressed with the "Right Now" presentation came back to me again and again. *The Daily Motivator* became one of the most popular places on the web for inspiring messages. Financially, my business went from just getting by to doing very well. I paid off that car years ahead of schedule.

No one wants bad things to happen. But they do happen on a regular basis. You can be going along great, following all the rules, working hard and doing your very best. Then out of nowhere, completely unexpectedly, circumstances can dramatically change through no fault of your own. When that happens, you have a choice. You can allow yourself to be pushed around by whatever is going on, and give up on your dream. Or, you can muster the strength to reach deep inside and reconnect with that dream, in a new and more meaningful way.

Your dream can always live on, no matter what. In fact, when you choose to keep it alive through all the ups and downs, no matter what, it grows ever stronger.

Those ups and downs certainly come. And just when you think things could not get worse, they get worse. Or just when you're about to pull ahead, something comes along and pushes you back. Is there any point in going on? Is it time to simply give up, to give in, to abandon your dreams, to turn your back on your most deeply held desires?

Absolutely not! No matter what has happened, no matter how difficult the conditions, no matter how much challenge is piled on top of challenge, there is always hope. In fact, the more difficult the situation, the more reason you have to move beyond it. The more you've lost, the less you have to lose and the more reason you have to stride confidently forward.

Even if you have nothing else, you have something more precious than the purest gold, a treasure more rare and desirable than the brightest diamond. You have life. You can sense. You can think. You can reason. You can make decisions. You can take action. Though you may lose all else, still you retain the ability to move yourself forward, to become the person you decide to become, to live in the way you have determined to live. And you still have your dream.

At times it may seem that the whole world is against you.

But that assessment is based on past history. And the past does not equal the future. The past does not equal the future because you stand solidly in the present, able to break away from whatever has happened in the past and to create your future in the way you desire.

When the setbacks come, reach inside and remind yourself why. Why do you value the things you value? Why do some things fill you with joy and other things make you incredibly sad? There is an unstoppable, driving purpose to your life. At times of great joy, at times of genuine excitement, at times of profound sorrow, you can feel that purpose. It is an intense experience to do so, and a reassuring one as well. Because it lets you know you are alive. There is a special meaning in this universe that exists in the person you are. Stay connected to that meaning. Stay focused on that purpose. Spend time with it. Get to know it. Seek to understand and enable it. Have fun with it!

Then, revived by your connection to the what and the why of your life, renew the commitment to move forward. Make it more powerful than ever. Renew your commitment to get up and take action. Renew your commitment to fulfill your most glorious possibilities.

Things will not always go as you planned. Things will not always work out the way you intended for them to. When that happens, you're fully capable of making the necessary adjustments and moving on ahead. There's no need to let the disappointments keep you down. Dwelling on disappointment comes from the mistaken belief that there is some value in being a victim. That is simply not true.

Instead of letting the setbacks set you back, decide to let them increase your determination. Channel the energy of your disappointment into the positive efforts of your comeback. When you've been knocked down, give yourself a pat on the back for making the effort, learn from the experience, then resolve to quickly get back in the game.

Every setback is temporary when you resolve to keep going. The greatest accomplishments happen when you get just a little way beyond the point where others would have quit. The difference between someone who enjoys magnificent success, and someone who just manages to get by, is the willingness to do whatever it takes, for as long as it takes, to reach the goal. You most certainly have it in you to do that.

Sit up straight. Stand up straight and tall. Take a deep breath. Walk with confidence in every step. Your physical posture and actions can strongly influence your level of effectiveness. Don't stand around and stare at the ground. You won't see anything that way. Lift your eyes up so you'll have room to view and comprehend the abundance of possibilities which can be yours. Smile. You can't remain discouraged for long when there's a genuine smile on your face.

When the going gets rough, and it seems like you just cannot take any more, remember—you can take it, you can make it, you can do it. All it ever takes is one step. One step in the direction of your goal. One step away from your troubles. Just one step. And then after that step, another. Anyone can take one step. Once you get back up and take that first step, and commit to taking the rest, things change. Momentum is suddenly on your side again. Soon the setback will be far behind you, and you'll be racing ahead faster than ever.

The Power of Ten Billion Dreams

Visualizing Your Dreams

Absolve you to yourself, and you shall have the suffrage of the world.

— Ralph Waldo Emerson

By connecting with a specific dream, and then making the commitment to bring that dream to life, you are creating an intention. The intention itself, however, is not enough. To give that intention real power, so your dream will indeed be fully manifested in your life, you have to connect it with your expectations. That creates a powerful combination. Whatever you expect to happen is going to happen. You are constantly in the process of creating your reality, all around you in your life, based on your expectations.

When you connect your dream with an authentic, unequivocal expectation, it will absolutely happen. Your dream will surely and faithfully unfold in your life.

How do you do that? How do you connect your dream to your expectations? You can do it through a powerful facility you already have. It's something you use every day, and you can take conscious control of this power. It is the power of visualization. Although visualization technically refers only to the sense of sight, we're speaking of it in broader terms here that include all your senses. It is the process of creating in your mind the full and rich sensory experience of the manifestation of your dream. It's not merely seeing things in your mind, but also hearing, feeling, touching, smelling and tasting the fulfillment of your dreams in your imagination. It is feeling the presence in all your senses, and feeling how it will be, how you will be, when your dream is fully realized.

This process of visualization is powerful in itself, and you can make it many times more powerful by repeating it over and over again in your mind. A great way to facilitate that is by creating stories for yourself of how your life will be when your dreams are fully realized.

The best way to explain the process is with an example. We'll use my dream of sailing from Texas to Barbados. The first step is to make the dream into a definite intention, by stating it in a positive manner in the present tense. That begins the process of installing it as an expectation. So, instead of saying something like "I hope someday I get the chance to sail to Barbados" I would say "I am sailing my own boat from Corpus Christi, Texas to the island of Barbados." Also, it is important to include in the intention some of the meaningful benefits of manifesting it. When your dream is authentic and comes from your true essence, that's no problem. In my case, one benefit of the sailing adventure will be the opportunity to spend quality time with good friends and family members onboard the boat. Preparing for and undertaking the journey will also challenge me to improve my sailing and navigation skills. Another benefit is that Karen and I will have the opportunity to make extended visits to some of our favorite Caribbean islands and also to explore other islands where we've not yet been. Plus, it will provide me with lots of time to read and to write more books.

Taking some of those things into consideration, I can make my statement of intention more powerful. So here's what it is:

"I am sailing my own boat from Texas to Barbados, creating great memories with family and friends while enjoying the islands of the Caribbean and gaining new inspiration for writing."

So, now that I have a statement of intention the next step is to connect it to my expectations. The intention by itself is not enough. I hear myself saying, "I am sailing my own boat from Texas to Barbados" but I don't really believe it. What I need now is to connect it with an expectation. The way to do that is through visualization. One of the most powerful forms of visualization is a story. And remember, this kind of visualization is concerned with more than just the visual sense. It is best when it employs a variety of senses in rich, meaningful and memorable ways. So what I'm going to do is to use the power of a story to lock my intention into my expectations. But I'm not just going to use one story. I'm going to greatly expand on the power by creating several different stories about various scenarios that I envision around my planned sailing adventure.

Now this is beginning to really sound like a lot of fun, so let's get started. First, I must come up with a specific scenario that could play out when my intention is realized, and make that scenario into a story, complete with plenty of details that appeal to the senses.

My first choice is to create a story about our daughters and their friends joining us for a portion of the trip. So, here goes:

Karen and I hurry to finish the BBQ Chicken pizza from the California Pizza Kitchen restaurant at Miami International Airport. Every other time we've eaten here it's been while waiting for a connecting flight. But we're not flying anywhere today. We're here to pick up our two daughters who are arriving on a flight from Houston. They're coming with their friends to join us for a sail across to Nassau, Bahamas and a week on the beach at Paradise Island. An announcement about a flight delay comes over the public address system, so we pause our conversation to listen. But it's not the flight we're meeting. That one is right on schedule, and due to land in about ten minutes. We get up and walk briskly to the baggage claim area. In one hallway the air conditioning system doesn't seem to be working. The warm, humid air makes me wish I was back on the boat, where I could just jump over the side into the water. Fortunately, it's nice and cool in the baggage claim area. Soon we spot our older daughter and her boyfriend. Right behind them is our younger daughter who is accompanied by one of her sorority sisters from college. Outside we hail a full size van taxi for the 6-mile ride to the marina. On the boat, by the time we get everyone settled in, it's 6:30 p.m. and the temperature is 89. I open a bottle of chilled Viognier and happy hour begins. In a little while the girls and their friends call a taxi to take them to South Beach for dinner, an excursion that Karen and I opt out of. Instead, we have some sandwiches and then I do one last check of the engine and the rigging as we watch a beautiful sunset. We're already asleep by the time the young people return at about 10:30 p.m. At six the next morning I'm awakened by the horn of a massive cruise ship coming into port at Dodge Island, just a mile or two away. The sky is clear, and there's a steady onshore breeze. It looks like a perfect day for beginning our sail to Nassau. I fire up the engine and get a brief whiff of diesel exhaust. Everyone else is still sleeping as I ease away from the dock and head east into Biscayne Bay. Our younger daughter is the first person to wake up. By that time, we've cleared the Biscayne Channel and are out in the Atlantic Ocean. She takes the wheel while I put the sails up. I cut the engine and let the wind carry us steadily along as the boat gently plows through the small waves. Soon, everyone else begins to appear in the cockpit, bringing orange juice, pop tarts and granola bars for breakfast. The air is thick with the aroma of sunscreen as our passengers prepare for a beautiful day in the tropics. Soon they are all up in front laying on the deck, soaking in the sun and listening to their iPods. Karen and I stay under the shade of the bimini, checking our bearing on the GPS. If this good wind continues, we'll easily make it to Nassau by tomorrow afternoon.

There you have it. That's one of several visualizations I have for the intention of sailing from Texas to Barbados. Notice that it is filled with sensory richness -- sights, sounds, aromas, touch and taste are all included. Also, the story makes several references to being with family members, since spending time with my family is one of the important reasons I have chosen the intention of making this trip. It's not a complicated story. It is really more of a pleasant vignette. Nonetheless, it is rich in sensory references. Plus, it is personally meaningful and easy to remember. Because it is so easy to remember, it is something I can call up in my mind at a moment's notice, and that's important. After all, the more often I tell this story to myself, the more power I give to the manifestation of my intention.

Having a couple more stories about the same intention will also serve to add immense power and momentum to bring that intention into reality. So I have created, for example, a story about Karen and me spending a few weeks in St. Martin, the island where we went on our honeymoon years ago. There's also a story about spending a day writing while anchored in Great Harbour near Peter Island, in the British Virgin Islands. Those stories, too, are filled with sensory richness and are connected directly to the "whys" of my dream—the personally meaningful reasons I have for making the journey. The point is to create stories that will bring the intention to life in my mind from several different perspectives, and carry that intention beyond my doubts into a place of positive expectation.

Now, it's your turn. Think about an authentic dream that you have for your life. Take the first step, and state that dream as a positive, present-tense intention. Then, create three stories, rich in sensory detail and personal meaning, that take place in the realm of your intention. If you have trouble coming up with those stories, or if you feel that you're not creative enough to imagine such stories, consider this. You tell yourself stories about your past all the time. Think for a moment about that. There are experiences in your past that you remember fondly, and can describe in great detail. Maybe sometimes you get together with old friends and re-live those memories. When you do, a part of you feels like you're there. You remember the way it looked. You remember the way it sounded. You remember the way the air felt, and the aromas that were present. You remember the camaraderie of your friends. You remember how good you felt while experiencing it.

And the thing is, you can be just as engaged and enthusiastic about some positive scenario that you envision in the future as you can be about the good things that have happened in your past. What's even better is that you can actually do something to make that imagined future scenario become real in your life.

To create stories about your intentions, you simply "remember" what has not yet happened with the same richness and meaning as you remember what you've already experienced. You absolutely have the capability of creating wonderfully rich and inspiring stories about what you intend to create for your life. In fact, you'll find it to be a very enjoyable exercise and really a whole lot of fun.

After you create your stories, replay them over and over again in your mind. That will transform your dream into a clear and powerful expectation. Once you do that, the magic begins. Because once you truly expect your intention, the energy of your life will move you in the direction of fulfilling that intention. All the little things you do each day will move you in that direction. Why is that so important? Because there are so very many thoughts and actions you have each day that you can't possibly control them all. However, when you have a powerful, positive expectation, the expectation itself takes control and leads you in the direction you expect to go. It exerts influence over both your conscious and subconscious decisions. Over time, as you maintain that expectation, you will naturally work to achieve it, often even without thinking about it. When you're driven by positive expectation, you don't have to try or struggle or force yourself to take positive, creative actions. They happen naturally. The creative, productive actions will easily flow from you to create the fulfillment of whatever you dream and truly expect.

Feeling the Fulfillment

If we could learn to like ourselves, even a little, maybe our cruelties and angers might melt away.
— John Steinbeck

I've used Apple Macintosh computers exclusively in my work and in my life since 1986. I know just about everything there is to know about the Mac, and then some. Lately, when I call Apple for tech support, I often end up assisting them more than they assist me. It's been more than a decade since I came across anyone at Apple who knew more about the Mac than I did. I say this not to brag, but to illustrate the fact that I am fascinated with understanding what makes things work.

Most people get a computer and want to know precisely which steps they should take to make the computer do what they want it to do. How do I write a letter on my letterhead? How do I print an envelope? How do I get on eBay? That kind of thing. For me, though, I want to know what's underneath the hood. Why does a word processing program save files in a particular folder by default, and how do I change that default? How is the "Time Machine" backup program able to save updated versions of all my files every hour without quickly running out of room on the hard drive? Why does a web form work correctly in one browser and not in another browser?

Back in the 1980s, Macintosh computers were pretty much a cult product. Real businesses used DOS (the predecessor to Windows). This was before the Internet was available to anyone other than nuclear physicists and their ilk. Back then, you either used DOS or you used Macintosh, and most everyone assumed that you could not share data between the two. Yet I quickly figured out a way to do exactly that. I used my Mac to do page layouts for newsletter and business brochures, and pretty much all of my customers used DOS computers. They would give me their material in a WordPerfect file on a 5¼ inch floppy disc, and I could zap that text into my Mac where I would do a beautiful layout.

The thing is, I love figuring out stuff like that. It all falls under the general category of logistics, which is just a fancy way of saying "figuring out how to get complicated stuff done, and then doing it."

One reason I'm attracted to sailing is because of the logistics involved. In sailing, there are a lot of complex issues that all have to come together to make it all work. There's the boat itself, and all its various structural and mechanical components. One big part of that is the engine, which always is in need of some kind of maintenance or repair. There's all sorts of rigging and wiring and plumbing and other things that have to work together. And the boat is just the beginning. For each journey, there's navigation, weather (which constantly changes), provisioning, tides, communication, mooring, docking, security and other such things to be planned, executed and tended to. Finally comes the logistics of having a good time, including food, music, wine and sightseeing arrangements. For some people, dealing with all these things might seem to be tedious and draining. For me, I can get so absorbed in them that I lose track of time.

Much of the attraction of an ambitious sailing trip to Barbados is in figuring out all the details that will make it happen, and then in tending to those details. It will be very challenging work, and yet to me it won't seem like work at all.

That same thing is true of the most powerful dreams. Confucius is quoted as saying, "Choose a job you love, and you will never have to work a day in your life." Dreams are difficult and challenging. Yet when you're living your dreams, it does not feel like work. It feels like fulfillment, because that's precisely what it is.

The Power of Ten Billion Dreams

From Someday to Now

What we call the secret of happiness is no more a secret than our willingness to choose life.

— Leo Buscaglia

Here's a seven-word sentence that encompasses everything you must do to really, truly live your dream:

Move your dream from someday to now.

It's fun to dream, to think about what you would like to do someday. But that someday part is a real problem. As long as you see your dream as occurring *someday*, it's not going to happen for you. Every person who has ever achieved a dream has done so by changing that dream from someday to now.

What's involved in doing that? Action. There is something you can do right now to begin living your dream. Of course that presents you with a real challenge. Are you serious about your dream or not? Do you truly want to live the reality of it, or do you just want to keep dreaming and wishing and hoping for it your entire life? If you're serious, there absolutely is something you can do right now, some very definite start you can make today.

Yes, I know about the excuses. You have all sorts of them. After all, if you didn't have all those excuses you would already be living the full and complete expression of your dream. But you're not. What enables you to keep your distance from your dream are those very impressive excuses.

There's not enough time. There's not enough money. You don't know anybody who could help you. Something's holding you back and it's not your fault. You're tired. You got off to a slow start. You have a slow metabolism. What else? Do any of these sound vaguely familiar?

The most powerful excuses are the ones that are true. Some excuses are just flat-out lies, and you know it, and those are pretty easy to get beyond. But the excuses that are real and valid and reasonable and true, those have the power to hold you back forever if you let them. The good news is, you don't have to let them.

Even though you have all sorts of great excuses, you can take action anyway. Even though there are plenty of totally valid reasons for not moving forward, you can move forward anyway. Here's a really clever way to do that. When you change your dream from someday to now, you can make an offsetting transaction. You can move your excuses from now to someday. Make your dreams and your excuses trade places! Once you do that, the excuses lose all their power. Because you move your excuses to someday, and someday never comes. It's never someday. It's always today.

What's so powerful about this little trick? It transforms the excuses that once held you back into powerful, compelling reasons for moving forward. For example, consider this all-too-common excuse:

"I don't have enough time."

Take that excuse and move it from now to someday. Here's what happens to it:

"Someday I won't have enough time."

So far, so good. It's no longer an excuse that you can use today. But there's more, and here's where it gets really interesting. Say the above sentence out loud to yourself. Go ahead. Do it. If there are people around and you're afraid you might be embarrassed, just whisper it under your breath. But go ahead and say the sentence, "Someday I won't have enough time."

Notice that when you say that sentence, it is pretty much impossible to stop at the end of it. The statement demands some kind of resolution. You feel an irresistible urge to put a "so" at the end, and to complete the thought. Go ahead and do it. Add the word "so" and then say whatever naturally comes to mind. Something like this:

"Someday I won't have enough time, so I'm making full use of the time I have today."

Not only have you nullified the excuse, you've transformed it into a compelling reason to get going. By moving the excuse from now to someday, you've changed it from a negative to a positive.

Do you have excuses? Lots of them? Great! Move them all to someday. And with the empty space that's now cleared out in this present day, put your dreams into action.

Whatever your dream may be, there is something you can do right now, some specific, positive action you can take, that will begin bringing that dream to life. The first step is right in front of you. You have everything it takes, right here, right now, to move your dream from someday to now. That first step will probably be a small one, and might seem insignificant. Yet there is great power in small actions that are repeated again and again.

Move your dream from someday to now.

What do you plan to do someday? Now is when you can go beyond planning and start doing. What dream would you like to be living someday? If it's good enough for someday, it's even better for today. Start living it now.

The amazing worldwide achievement machine gives you countless ways to take action. What you once considered someday has now arrived. This is when you can actually begin to live your dream. This is when you have the enjoyable opportunity of creating the value that's meaningful to you.

Move your dream from someday to now. Make it a mantra. "I've moved my dream from someday to now." Remind yourself often. The dream is here and now, for you to live.

Living that dream requires real, sustained effort. At the heart of living your dream, is action.

Actually, though, that's the easy part. It will be challenging, inconvenient and often complicated, as well as tedious and frustrating at times. Yet the effort itself, as challenging as it may be, is the easy part, once you get started on it. The difficult part is getting yourself to do it, and staying committed to it.

Think about it. Have there been times when you resisted doing something, or going somewhere, or talking to someone because it just seemed like it would be so difficult? And then, when you finally had to break down and do it, the task was not nearly as bad as you expected. In fact, once you got started you realized that you actually were enjoying yourself. And then you regretted not doing it sooner.

The work itself is not all that difficult, once you make your mind up to do it. A journey of a thousand miles seems impossible before you begin it. Yet once you start, you realize that all you have to do is take one step at a time. Take just one small, simple step. Then, take the next one, and the next. Even the longest journey, even the greatest achievement, even the most magnificent dream that you can dare to dream, is built one little step at a time.

In 1997 I published my first book, *The Daily Motivator To Go.* At that time I had written approximately 500 daily messages, and I selected about 250 of them to include in the book. In the introduction I wrote:

> The book you hold in your hands is a testament to the value of persistence and consistent effort. It was not written as a book, but rather as a series of daily messages, day after day after day. And not only was that the *method,* it is also a key *message* of this book. You can accomplish anything, *anything,* when you consistently apply effort for as *long as it takes.*

Writing a whole book seems like a daunting task, and it can be. However, writing a half dozen brief paragraphs each day is much more approachable and far easier to imagine yourself doing. That's what I did, and soon I had more than enough material for an entire book.

The stumbling block is not the work itself. You're absolutely capable of doing what must be done, or of contracting with someone to do it for you. You're also completely capable of figuring out what has to be done. After all, you're built from the ground up for achievement, for making a difference, for getting things done. The stumbling block is getting yourself to do it. You have to make the commitment to get the work done.

That's why it is crucial that your dreams are truly yours. That's why it is essential for you to be completely clear about why you have chosen to live and to fulfill each of those dreams. The dreams you accomplish are the dreams that come from your purpose. Those are the dreams you'll be unable to ignore. Those are the dreams that will get you out of bed every morning. Those are the dreams that will give you no choice but to make one more phone call, knock on one more door, write one more email, take one more lap around the track, make one more effort, and then do it again and again until you achieve what you have chosen to achieve.

The Power of Ten Billion Dreams

An authentic dream will give you instant discipline. A friend of mine had been struggling with a weight problem for years. Then one day in October her daughter became engaged to be married, with a wedding date set for the next June. Suddenly, this person acquired unshakable discipline when it came to diet and exercise. She had a driving desire to get in shape and look great for the wedding. She had a real, authentic dream that she knew was well within her ability to achieve, if she just did certain things each day. She kept the dream at the forefront of her awareness. Instead of continuing to struggle with her weight, she instantly had the discipline to do something about it. When the wedding day arrived, she had lost more than 30 pounds, enabling her to thoroughly enjoy her role as mother of the bride.

Everyone has the ability for discipline in them. You have the ability to act with persistence and rock solid discipline. A dream that is truly yours will activate and maintain that discipline. Move that dream from someday to now, and begin to benefit from its treasures.

The Power of Ten Billion Dreams

Touch Points

Visualize this thing that you want, see it, feel it, believe in it.
Make your mental blue print, and begin to build.
— Robert Collier

One very powerful way to literally move your dream from someday to now is by creating touch points. What are touch points? As an example, let me explain one of mine.

I dream of sailing the Caribbean. I dream of anchoring my sailboat in a beautiful, peaceful spot, and sitting in the cockpit, in the shade of a nice, big fabric Bimini cover, while working on my next book. I dream of being able to, when I get hot, jump into the refreshing water of the Caribbean Sea for a leisurely swim to cool off and to gather my thoughts. And right now, today, at my home in Austin, Texas, as I write these words, I'm living that dream. I'm absolutely feeling that dream, not just in my imagination, but with all of my senses. In fact, I'm feeling it so intensely I know without a doubt it is absolutely happening. Why is that?

Though I am not currently on a sailboat, and I'm hundreds of miles away from the islands of the Caribbean, I'm still able to experience much of what I dream of experiencing. I'm sitting in the shade of a dark green fabric patio umbrella, typing this chapter on my MacBook computer. About four steps away is the swimming pool. The air temperature is currently 95 degrees, and a few minutes ago, after finishing a long, difficult chapter that I had been working on for weeks, I was getting a little bit hot, plus I wanted to take a break. So I jumped in the pool and swam laps for about 15 minutes. It felt absolutely wonderful and it completely revived me, just as I know will happen when I'm writing on my sailboat and jump overboard for a quick swim. In fact, as I was swimming today, passing by the lush sago palms that surround the pool, I closed my eyes and it was quite easy to imagine myself swimming back and forth beside my boat off the west coast of Barbados. I checked the little yellow floating thermometer with the rubber-ducky head. It showed the pool water temperature to be 84 degrees, which is a perfect temperature for a refreshing break on such a warm day. That made me curious. Once I got out of the pool and dried off, I opened up the MacBook and checked the Internet. According to the website surf-forecast.com, the sea surface temperature today near the west coast of Barbados is precisely the same, 84 degrees Fahrenheit.

There's a gentle breeze swaying the branches of the palms, the sky is a beautiful blue, the sun is shining brightly, and here I am in the middle of it all, under the shade of a fabric cover, doing what I love, having just taken a cool, refreshing swim. All of those things would be precisely the same whether I was in the islands or in my backyard. The dream is absolutely real, and I'm absolutely inspired to continue allowing it to unfold through my efforts.

My backyard scenario is a touch point that evokes the reality of my dream. Such touch points can be extremely powerful because they enable you to literally feel the substance of your dream throughout all of your being.

For any dream you have, there is something you can do right now to really, truly live the experience of that dream. It can be highly motivating to know you're working toward the fulfillment of your dream. However, it is much more motivating when you're actually experiencing key elements of your dream in your current situation, with all of your senses.

In an earlier chapter, we looked at how every dream is a dream about how you wish to feel. Though it is important to be specific about the people, places, experiences and things in your dream, it is also important to remember that at the heart of your dream is your purpose.

At the heart of my dream of sailing to Barbados, is my purpose of encouraging as many people as possible to live their best possibilities. The part about sailing to Barbados resonates with things I love and value. I know that by undertaking the journey I will find the inspiration to bring my work to higher and higher levels of effectiveness.

The great thing is, I don't have to be that far along with the fulfillment of my dream to begin reaping the benefits of the dream. In fact, I can begin to enjoy the benefits immediately. I can feel how the tropical breeze will feel, I can feel the warm sun on my skin, I can feel the cool water as I dive into it, and I can feel my inspiration growing ever stronger. I can do all this just by focusing on my dream and stepping out into my backyard.

For every dream, there are powerful touch points that you can access immediately. With a little imagination and creativity, you can come up with touch points for your own dream.

Do you dream, for example, of living in a certain part of town? In fact, you can live there right now. No, you may not be in a position to maintain a residence there, but you can still live there. You can drive over to that part of town and take a long walk every day. You can shop at the stores in that part of town. You could take your children to play at a park in that part of town. You could even join a church or other organization in the part of town where you dream of living. Though you may not be sleeping every night in that part of town, you can still be living significant portions of your life there. By doing that, you'll be inspiring yourself to take the steps necessary for buying or renting a residence there.

Or perhaps you dream of working in a particular industry. This very day, you can get on the Internet and learn all you can about that industry. You can find out what kinds of challenges face the people working in that industry, and work on devising solutions to those challenges. If you do that, guess what? You'll actually be working in that industry. No, you may not have a paying job, but you'll be gaining the kind of valuable experience that will eventually enable you to get a great job.

Touch points are real. They connect you in a solid, visceral way to the substance of your dream. A touch point is not an exercise in faking it until you're making it. Rather, a touch point enables you to truly feel the reality of your dream. Dreams are all about feelings, and good touch points give you the opportunity to feel the fulfillment of your dream even as you are working to achieve that fulfillment. Find yourself some good touch points, and enjoy living your dream so much that you'll do whatever is necessary to bring it into complete fulfillment.

But...

You are never too old to set another goal or to dream a new dream.

— C.S. Lewis

What you're saying is great, Ralph, but... I lost my job. Or, I'm so deep in debt I can't possibly make enough money each month to pay it off. I'm going further and further in the hole. My investments have all been wiped out. I'm sick. I have a serious, chronic disease. I can't follow my dream because of my situation. I have a financial problem or a family problem. My son is a drug addict and I've got to deal with that. And anyway, I'm too old.

So... what you're saying about dreams sounds nice. Maybe if I was just starting out, or if I were making more money, or if I didn't have all these family obligations, it would be nice to follow my dream, but I just can't.

What can you offer me? I can't do it. I don't have the money or the time. Get the picture?

The answer to that is this...

Yes, I understand. I understand you have challenges, obligations, things that prevent you from spending all your time in the way you choose. But here's what you have the complete freedom to do. You can always put into your mind whatever you choose to put into your mind. Even though you may have a chronic illness, even though you may have lost your job, even though you may owe huge amounts of money, even though you may have a child who is in trouble and needs your help, even though life is difficult and tough and even painful, still your very best option is to fill your mind and your spirit with the power of a positive dream, with the power of what you really, truly would like to do with your life, and with the power of the essential purpose that comes from the heart of you.

Even though things are tough, and you have to spend all day working three jobs, and you can't possibly imagine how you would ever be able to reach your dream, even though you can't imagine how, here's the thing. The how is not what's important. No, you absolutely cannot contemplate how you would ever reach what you're dreaming of. Let's go ahead and accept the fact that you can't figure out how to do it. From where you are, given your circumstances, it realistically appears totally impossible for you. Even so, your best option is to dream it.

Because, the thing is, life doesn't stand still. Life changes. And something else changes. You change. Your perspective changes. The way things are today is not the way they will be tomorrow. The way the world is today is not the way the world will be tomorrow.

I could not have imagined how to get to where I am now. I used to dream of being able to write for a living, and make a good living at it. But I couldn't imagine how that was going to happen. I really couldn't. Yes, I could envision living it, someday, in the future. But I could not see the specifics of how I would get there. What I could do was dream, and start to work on the part of that dream, however small, that I could work on. I had some time to write, and I had the desire to write, so I started doing it. I just started doing it.

I didn't even think that the small steps I was taking at the time would really lead to any place of any consequence. I just wanted to do it. I had a passionate desire to do it. And so I did.

Now, it has earned me millions of dollars. My writing and the things associated with it, have indeed worked out. Actually, it hasn't worked out. I've worked it out. I've worked at it, diligently and persistently, for years, for long hours, for weeks at a stretch without doing much else. Many of the best things I've written, including large sections of this book, have been written outside next to my pool late at night on my laptop computer by the light of a couple of citronella torches. So quite literally, I have been burning the midnight oil, so much so that I usually purchase citronella oil by the case.

It hasn't been easy. It has required a lot of work and it still does. But the thing is, there was a way. I didn't know it at the time when I started, but I did start. There was a way to get from A to B. I couldn't see the details of that path at first. But once I started taking the first steps, once I started putting commitment and action into it, it unfolded. It unfolded and I kept at it.

You may be sitting at the point where you cannot imagine how it could be possible. Maybe you think you're too old and there's not enough time left. Maybe you feel that you're so deep in financial debt that there's no way, even if you worked 100 hours a week or more for years and years, no way you could ever pay off that debt and get to where you want to be.

But I'm telling you that such thinking is linear thinking. And the thing is, life is not linear. Thank goodness! Consider all the assumptions you're making now. Some of them aren't going to be valid in as short a time as a couple of weeks.

There is a way. Life is not linear. It can be exponential. I created a web presentation and shared it with a few hundred people, and most of them shared it with other people, and soon there were millions of people who had seen it. Most of that exposure, I did not create myself. It was not a linear thing. I didn't contact a million people and ask each of them to look at the presentation. I never could have done that. But they saw it. It was an exponential growth, one person telling two or three others, and each of them telling a few others, and so on. That kind of thing grows quickly, a lot faster than you can do all by yourself. And that's just one example. The point is, things can happen more powerfully than you can contemplate them happening. There are forces that align in your favor that you may not ever even be aware of, but that can help you immensely. What is it that summons these forces? Your authentic passion and commitment.

Whatever you can dream is possible and realistic. It may not be realistic in the exactly the way you envision it. In fact, it probably isn't. However, the real substance of your dream is possible and realistic. The way you desire to feel when living that dream is absolutely possible and realistic.

We like to think we're very logical and realistic, but we only know about a small fraction of reality. There's a lot more reality going on than we can ever know about. When it comes to your dreams, don't get caught up in making judgments about what's possible, or what's practical, or what's realistic. Instead, use that energy to feel your dream. Feel it and begin to live it.

Even if your dream never is fully realized, it's still much better for you to follow that dream than to ignore or discount it. You're still better off right now when you start working your way toward it. What if you just get ten percent of it? What if you just get five percent of it? Well, that's better off than you were before, isn't it?

The moment you start working toward your dream, the moment you really commit to that dream, and begin to live it with all you have, the moment you do that you begin to benefit from it. You begin to see the rewards of the dream in your life immediately. It doesn't take years. It doesn't require certain conditions to be in place. That dream immediately begins to improve you from the inside out. You begin to feel it, maybe not fully, but you do begin to feel its positive power. And not only does that continually move you toward your dream, it can improve everything about your life. It makes you more positively focused, more purposeful, and more effective at everything you do.

Let's say you dream to travel the world, but you're never able to fulfill that dream. Still, you're going to learn plenty about the world and about how to get around in it in the process of working and living toward your dream. Perhaps your dream is to travel to China. So you learn all you can about China. Maybe you even learn how to speak the language. And then you don't get to make the trip. Well, are you better off than if you had never dreamed? Yes! You know all about China. You know the language. That's immensely valuable. If somebody else wanted to go to China, that person could call you up and you could give them valuable advice. You could become a China travel consultant. You could probably make money at it.

The point is, no matter where you're starting from, no matter what you perceive as your chance of reaching the dream, you're better off with it than without it. No matter what happens with that dream, whether you reach it or not, you're better off having it and living toward it than not. Now of course it's vitally important that your dream is authentic. It is essential for your dream to be something that truly fulfills your purpose. When it is, you're going to get valuable benefits from it, and you're going to get some of those benefits almost immediately. Yes, of course it would be great for that dream to be fully realized, and when you're fully committed to it, the odds are good that it will happen. But even if it doesn't, the dream still has great value to you. You don't have to wait until it's all finished. The minute you start living toward your dream, you begin to benefit.

It doesn't matter what has happened or where you're coming from. The way to immediately put value in your life is to live your dream.

The Power of Ten Billion Dreams

Integrity
and Forgiveness

You cannot do wrong and feel right. It is impossible!
— Ezra Taft Benson

It's great for you to follow your dream, whatever that dream may be. Even if it is frivolous or self-serving or impractical, your dream can bring outstanding value to all of life.

However, if you're not careful you can cheat yourself and the whole world out of the value of your dream. That happens when you get the misguided notion that you can find a shortcut to the fulfillment of your dream. That's impossible, because the essence of your dream is in the authentic living of it, and there simply is no shortcut. A whole lot of people try to find them, though.

By far, the two most common attempted shortcuts are expecting something for nothing and taking advantage of other people. Often these two perceived shortcuts are combined together. Both are based on the completely false assumption that your dream can be fulfilled for you by someone or something outside of you. Again, that's impossible.

Millions of people buy lottery tickets regularly. Only a very, very few people end up, over time, winning more than what they pay to play. Only a tiny percentage of that already small percentage actually win the large jackpot amounts. And most of those big jackpot winners end up back where they started financially after only a few years.

Winning a lot of money or taking it from someone else will not fulfill your dreams. Only you can fulfill your dreams. To do that, you must choose to live with integrity. Without integrity, it all falls apart.

Yes, absolutely do whatever you must do to bring your dream to life, but don't expect something for nothing. Don't think you can get there by taking advantage of other people.

Don't cheat. Don't steal. Don't lie. Don't compromise your integrity in order to follow your dream. That doesn't help anyone. Obviously it doesn't help the person you're scheming to take advantage of. It doesn't help the world at large. And it doesn't even help you. In fact it does great harm not only to everyone else, but also to you. If you compromise your integrity, you're creating a world for yourself in which dreams are impossible to achieve. The amazing worldwide achievement machine runs on dreams. It powerfully enables the fulfillment of dreams of all kinds. And it is maintained by integrity. Without integrity, it all breaks down.

If we can't trust each other, if we are suspicious of each other all the time, we won't ever get anything done. It's perfectly fine for everyone to be looking out for himself or herself. It's not fine to do so at the expense of other people.

Some people see this as a zero-sum world. They think that one person must lose if another person is to win. That assumption is flat out wrong, and it creates two big problems. It causes some people to blame their failures on others, and it causes other people to seek to take advantage of others in order to succeed. It breeds envy, resentment, and vengeance, none of which add value to life. The amazing worldwide achievement machine begins to sputter to a halt whenever mistrust, deceit, and greed are fed into it.

Wait a minute. Greed? Isn't greed the same as self-interest? Haven't we seen that self-interest is good, and productive, and ultimately in the best interest of everyone?

In fact, greed is not the same as self-interest, no matter how successful and expansive that self-interest may be. There's a common misconception that greed means taking more than one's fair share. But that definition of greed depends on the zero-sum mentality I just mentioned. The universe in which we live is endlessly abundant. There is no end to the value that can be expressed and experienced. So each and every person's fair share is infinite. That makes it impossible for you, or for anyone else, to acquire more than a fair share. What is greed, then? Greed is the expectation of something for nothing. Greed is seeking to harm or to take advantage of others. And wherever it is tried, it fouls up the gears of the amazing worldwide achievement machine.

Yes, honest competition is great. Bullying is not. Effective and efficient production is good. Stealing is a whole different matter. Promoting new and innovative goods and services is great. Lying, misrepresenting, and intentionally deceiving people are whole different matters. Such behavior is not competition. Competition is doing your best with what you have. Lying, stealing and cheating are not a part of healthy, productive competition.

So yes, follow your dream. Follow your dream, whatever it is. But don't deceive yourself into thinking you can compromise your integrity. You cannot live the fullness and richness of your dream, without your integrity.

Do you realize how much trust is worth? If you can trust someone else, you don't have to keep checking up on that person. You don't have to question everything that person tells you to make sure it's true. You don't have to double-check and verify. You can trust that person. It saves you an enormous amount of time and energy. You can ask the person to do something and have confidence it will be done. That's extremely valuable. That's what employers look for when hiring employees. They're looking for people they can trust to carry out the tasks they ask those people to do. So quite literally, people are willing to pay for the ability and opportunity to trust others.

Trust is enormously important. It's not only being trustworthy that's so important, but also having people you can trust. It's essential to cultivate trust in both directions. Trust is highly valued and valuable, and trust grows from acting with integrity. So if you desire to have more value in your life, if you wish to live in a world that's filled with meaningful value, then you must have trust. That trust grows from acting with integrity.

What does the word mean, integrity? Literally, integrity means being whole and undivided. It means that every aspect of your life is in harmony with the whole. When something has integrity, it holds together well. All the parts are supporting each other. It's consistent. Living with integrity means that the values in your life and your entire existence are consistent throughout all of your life and all of your world. When you have integrity, you treat others as you would like to be treated, because you acknowledge that we're all connected.

Integrity recognizes the fact that we're all connected. Here's a simple, powerful way to always live with integrity. Just remind yourself that you cannot harm others without harming yourself, and you cannot help others without also helping yourself.

We've talked a lot about how it's your obligation to enjoy life. In fact, in my opinion, as I've explained, that's why we're here. We're here to fully enjoy the experience of living. That's what we're good at. That's what resonates with our spirit—enjoying life. But that absolutely doesn't mean it's ok to take advantage of other people in order to enjoy life. In the end, it simply is not enjoyable.

After all, do you really want to take pleasure in someone else's pain? Well, maybe you want to out of a sense of revenge, perhaps if that other person has caused you pain in the first place. It's understandable. But even though it's understandable, it doesn't lead to anywhere good. Here's what's much better than revenge. Forgiveness.

With forgiveness, instead of putting all your energy in to perpetuating all the negative things that have happened, you free that energy to do more useful and valuable things. Revenge just extends and amplifies the negativity. Even if you're able to extract revenge, you don't end up with anything that's going to add value to your life. You really haven't even broken even. You've just perpetuated the hurt, and you've used up a lot of time and effort to do it.

Yes, the hurt can be very bad and it is entirely appropriate for people to experience punishment for their transgressions, for the evil and hateful things they do. But you don't have to be the agent of that punishment. That's just a continuation of the hurt. It adds nothing positive to your life. Yes, perhaps it's a necessary thing. It is appropriate that people receive punishment for their misdeeds because that will discourage them from repeating the behavior. Even so, carrying out punishment isn't the thing you would choose if you had other choices with what to do with your life. And you do have many other choices.

The Power of Ten Billion Dreams

You may have a desire to see another person punished if you've been hurt very badly by that person. That's understandable. But the whole point here is that forgiveness, for you, from your perspective, is always the best choice. Always. For you.

True, it may not always be possible. There may be times when you decide that forgiveness is not warranted, that punishment and revenge are appropriate to pursue. Even so, forgiveness is always the best choice, from the perspective of what it will bring to your life. Forgiveness frees you. When you can truly forgive, you are free of the hurt. There may still be residual effects of whatever happened. If someone stole all your money, you're still broke after forgiving that person. Yet when you forgive, you can stop putting your energy into being upset, angry and vengeful. You can start putting your energy into moving forward and into doing something about being broke.

That is the power of forgiveness. It lets you move past those who have wronged you, and frees you to live your dreams.

Forgiveness and integrity sound like very altruistic values, and they are. Yet they are also highly self serving, in a very positive way. Your integrity helps you more than it helps anyone else. Your forgiveness benefits your life more than it benefits anyone else.

Your dream is too valuable. Don't cheat yourself out of it. Live with integrity. Practice forgiveness. And bring your best dreams fully to life.

The Power of Ten Billion Dreams

Gratitude

Gratitude is not only the greatest of virtues, but the parent of all the others.

— Marcus Tullius Cicero

Look out at the world and what do you see? Abundance. In every direction, in countless forms, on every day and in every situation, a limitless supply of abundance surrounds you. In just one drop of water is enough atomic energy to power your car for a hundred thousand miles. Yet all the energy in all the water in all the oceans of the world cannot equal the living energy of your spirit. With that energy, you can do anything. You can harness as much of life's abundance as necessary and transform it into meaningful value.

How do you feel about that? I suggest you feel immensely thankful, all the time.

Life has its problems and challenges, to be sure. Yet those problems are overwhelmingly outnumbered by the positive possibilities. You can lose everything you have. Yet you can gain much, much more than you have. The downside is limited. The upside potential has no limit.

Living your dream is really a matter of transforming life's limitless abundance into a form that has meaning and value to you. What is it that keeps you connected to that abundance? Gratitude.

The abundance is ready and waiting for you, and there's more of it all the time. Yet if you cannot see that abundance, or if you have the slightest doubt about its existence, then it might as well not be there. Gratitude is what will open your eyes to the abundance, and keep your thoughts focused upon it.

When you are sincerely thankful for what you already have, then what you have becomes much more valuable and useful to you. In fact, what you already have is everything necessary to begin reaching the fulfillment of anything you can dare to dream. With thankfulness in your heart, you can clearly see that. In choosing to be thankful for whatever may come, you're able to fashion a completely realistic and workable way forward, all the way to the full manifestation of your dream.

If you spend your time and attention being dissatisfied with the way things are, then what you end up with is even more dissatisfaction. Whatever you focus upon, grows more abundant in your life. If you focus upon how cruel and unjust the world is, then you will encounter much more cruelty and injustice. If you constantly think about how much you hate your job, your working conditions will become even more unpleasant.

Gratitude, on the other hand, moves your world in a positive direction. Even if you can't stand your job, there is some reason why you keep going to work. There's something to be thankful for. There are some positive, desirable qualities to that job. Challenge yourself to figure out what they are. Most likely, one positive quality is that you get paid for working, and then you can spend the money on whatever you wish to spend it on. So obviously that's something right there to be thankful for. In addition, some of the things you do in connection with your job probably give you a sense of accomplishment. Plus, the job provides you with valuable experience. Even if you work with people who are impossibly difficult, every day you're becoming more highly skilled at working with difficult people, and that's a very useful skill to have.

The point here is that in any situation you can find certain aspects of that situation to be thankful for. Gratitude is always possible. Just as importantly, gratitude is always valuable. Every time, gratitude makes the whole situation more positive and useful to you and to the fulfillment of your dream. Gratitude magnifies and expands upon the positive aspects of any circumstance.

The more thankful you are for what you have, the more effectively you can make use of it. You are already immersed in and connected to life's great supply of abundance. Gratitude provides you with awareness and control over that connection, and enables you to transform that abundance into the life of your dreams.

Pick up your cell phone, or click your computer's mouse,

and you're instantly connected to the amazing worldwide achievement machine. Do you understand how immensely powerful that is? Any wealthy industrialist from 150 years ago would have given his entire fortune for that kind of power, and you carry it around in your pocket every day. Focus your gratitude on that, and feel the possibilities come popping into your mind.

Your most treasured dream is close enough to touch. With an ever-thankful heart, reach out, touch that dream, and bring it fully to life.

A Day in the Life of My Dream

I dream for a living.

— Steven Spielberg

Early on a Saturday morning in mid October, just before the sun comes up, we back out of the garage. The weather forecast is for a gloriously beautiful day, with highs in the low 80s and a dry southwest wind. There's not a cloud in the sky. Our destination is Kemah, a coastal town on the shore of Galveston Bay. We're going shopping for a boat. We're stepping forward to live the dream. From our home in Austin, it's about a four-hour drive so we're getting an early start.

The gas gauge shows only about a quarter of a tank. We won't make it on that. So before we leave the neighborhood, I stop to fill up. Karen goes inside to get a couple bottles of cold water for the road. I stay outside and operate the self-serve pump that puts fuel in our car. Where does that fuel come from? A tanker truck driver delivered it a few days ago. He's twenty-seven years old, married, with a baby boy. His dream is to own a whole fleet of trucks. My purchase of gasoline helps, in a small yet significant way, to nourish that dream.

We arrive in Kemah about lunchtime, and decide to get a bite to eat at a local restaurant. Karen orders a grilled chicken sandwich and I get a shrimp po boy. Our waitress, whose name is Carolyn, tells us that her daughter is a student at The University of Texas Medical Branch at Galveston, pursuing her dream of being a doctor. Carolyn works during the week in the office at an oil refinery. On weekends, and some evenings, she works as a waitress to help pay her daughter's medical school expenses. The food is great, the service is even better, and we leave a big tip.

Then comes the really fun part. We've found six pre-owned boats for sale that we've arranged with a couple of different yacht brokers to look at, plus we're visiting with another dealer about purchasing a brand new Beneteau model. He has a 49-foot model for us to look at, though that particular one is a good bit beyond our price range. It doesn't hurt (or cost anything) to look, though.

We spend the afternoon climbing down companionways, laying down on sleeping berths, rocking gimbaled stoves, checking out rigging, and peering into engine compartments. On each boat, I sit in the cockpit with one hand on the wheel, and imagine ourselves gently gliding through the warm, blue waters of the Caribbean. I can feel the dream coming to life.

One of the yacht brokers takes a real interest in us. He's in his late sixties. In a former life, he was a corporate executive who owned a charter sailboat in the British Virgin Islands. He and his family used to spend three weeks every February sailing through the islands. Several times, they took their boat down island, and once went all the way to Grenada. Though they never went to Barbados, they did sail to nearby St. Lucia, and he is very interested in the journey we are planning. He gives us all sorts of advice about the various options relating to hull designs and rigging, plus some excellent tips on electronics and navigation gear. At the age of 58, he had to sell his boat and start over financially. The company he had worked for was involved in an accounting scandal. Not only did he lose his high-paying corporate job, but his retirement account was wiped out. So he went with what he loved, sailing. It has taken him many years, but he's now back on his feet. In addition to brokerage, he does instruction for bareboat certification and even does some consulting for racing teams. More importantly, he's living his dream and having the time of his life. We decide that no matter which boat we end up buying, we definitely want to buy it through him if possible.

As the sky grows dark, we're heading into Houston, where we have a reservation at a hotel that's near our oldest daughter's apartment. Our plan is to pick her up and take her to dinner, but first we go and check into the hotel to get cleaned up. The young lady at the front desk asks how our day was, so I tell her about looking at all the sailboats in Kemah. It turns out that she and her husband are leaving in a few weeks for a Windjammer Cruise in the Bahamas, something they've dreamed of doing for years.

On the surface, my dream of sailing to Barbados seems like such a frivolous thing. After all, in some ways it's nothing more than an extended tropical vacation. And yet, even in its infancy, as I begin to take the first steps toward it, even in just one day, that dream has connected with and supported and nourished many other dreams. This particular dream of mine is something that I've always wanted to do. It's not any kind of grand strategy to save the world. And yet, the more I act on that dream, the more value it brings to the world, even long before the dream is fully realized.

Every authentic dream has the power to raise a little corner of the world by just a little bit. It doesn't matter whether or not the dream explicitly involves being of service to others. For as that dream is realized, it cannot help but make a positive difference in the lives of many people. What matters is that the dream has real meaning, and that it is acted upon with persistence and determination. One dream at a time, life grows richer, even more dreams are enabled, and the world moves relentlessly forward.

The Power of Ten Billion Dreams

What's Missing

Every man is a consumer, and ought to be a producer.
He is by constitution expensive, and needs to be rich.
— Ralph Waldo Emerson

It's all here. It's all around you—the amazing worldwide achievement machine.

The factories are here. The communication networks are here. The resources are here. The knowledge is here. The information is here. The technology is here. The ability to move people and things from place to place is here. The energy is here.

What's missing?

What is it that will take all this stuff, all these systems, all these capabilities and create the real, meaningful value the world so desperately requires? What is it?

What's missing is something to give it life. What's missing is the input of authentic purpose. What's missing is your dream. What the world needs, more than anything, is your dream, and my dream, and the dream of the person next to you, and the dreams of all the people in your town, the dreams of all the people in your country, the dreams of people all over the world. What will make positive and life-enriching use of all we have is the power of ten billion dreams.

Dreams will lead to the creation of great and useful things that have never been created before. Dreams can take all the skills, capabilities, knowledge and resources we have and transform them into new and meaningful value.

Dreams and the meaningful value they bring—that's what we can always use much more of. We have everything else. We've developed an amazingly productive society. The profound economic problems we face, individually and collectively, do not stem from the lack of ability to produce. On the contrary, we can produce in great quantity. We can literally overwhelm the Earth with production. What's missing is *meaningful* production. What's sorely missing—the source of many of our most difficult problems—is the fact that what we're producing is not what we really desire.

The world's problems are never going to be solved by a bunch of self-proclaimed intellectuals gathering together and coming up with grand schemes. That kind of approach can only lead to tyranny, with a select few people telling other people how to live.

All people have a yearning to be free. That yearning is well placed, because all people also have the ability to be free, to connect with what is meaningful and to work their way through whatever challenges come along. Look at places in the world where there is extreme poverty and what you'll find are people who are not free to address their own challenges. Look at places in the world where there is great prosperity and you'll also find abundant personal freedom. When people are free to act in their own, authentic self-interest while also respecting the lives of others, life can be highly fulfilling. When people are free to fulfill their own desires by acknowledging and supporting the desires of others, meaningful achievement is a way of life.

That's where dreams come in. Dreams tell you what you really desire. They're not selfish, any more than being alive is selfish. In fact, real, authentic dreams are the opposite of selfish. Dreams represent the unique value you possess, that you can give to the world. Dreams enable you to express the meaning of life in a way that's original and compelling. In our world today we have an elaborate and powerful infrastructure set up to fulfill dreams, and what it requires, are dreams to fulfill.

Nobody can live your dreams for you. It's hard work. It's something you must do yourself. It's difficult. It's uncomfortable. It exposes you.

Yet it also fulfills you. Living your dreams is what you're all about. It goes to the very core of you, and pulls out that spark of creation that lives within you—that eternal spark of creation that let's you know you're alive, that lets you know that you are, that lets you know you exist, and that all of creation exists.

Aren't you tired of just having stuff? Aren't you tired of having a lot of meaningless activity in the service of that meaningless stuff? All that energy can be put into something that will bring your life great fulfillment rather than frustration and despair. Think of all the energy you put out every second of every day. Imagine putting all that energy into joy, into beauty, into meaning and fulfillment and purpose. Imagine that.

You deserve the best life has to offer and you deserve the experience of creating it. There's really no other way to get the best that life has to offer if you're not the person who brings it into your life. No one else can give you fulfillment. Because by its very definition, fulfillment is something you have the opportunity to do yourself. If you don't do it yourself, it's not really fulfillment. It might be impressive to other people. It might look good on your résumé. It might get you noticed in the world, but it's not going to be real fulfillment. It may get you a lot of friends, but it's not going to be real fulfillment for you.

Your own fulfillment, the real richness of living, comes when you give of yourself. It comes when you make use of your own unique skills, when you tap into your own unique interests and passions. That's what will bring you fulfillment. And you deserve that. You deserve the very best. You must not let anyone take that away from you under the guise of trying to make life easier for you. Fulfillment is difficult, but that's great. Because in that difficulty is the value. In that hard work is the sense of accomplishment you'll get by bringing richness into your own life, by giving of yourself.

Yes, you deserve a life that is full of the very best. It's great to help other people. It's great to work together with other people and get help from other people, to work in cooperation with those around you. That's wonderful. That's what we're all here to do, to help each other. But the thing is, no one can give you the fulfillment that will bring that richness to your life. People can give you advice. People can give you assistance. People can give you the opportunity. People can give you a break. But you're the one who has to make it happen in order for it to mean anything.

You're the one. You deserve it. So make it happen. Use this moment right now. Use what you have. Tap into your value, the value inside of you. Tap into the power of your dreams.

The Power of Ten Billion Dreams

Imagine once again the most wonderful thing you've ever felt, and multiply it by ten. And then multiply it again by a hundred. That's what's possible. And not only is it possible, it's your obligation. It's your obligation to the creation of which you're a part. It's your duty to the unfathomable series of events and energies that went into bringing you to this point where you are right now. It's your special purpose to live a life that's fulfilled, that's full, and that has meaning.

No, it's not all fun and games. And yet, it's always possible to live with a deep and abiding sense of joy, a joy at knowing that you're whole, and that you're in resonance with all that is, in harmony with all that is.

The thing is, all of life exists to fulfill your dream. All of life exists to fulfill your authentic dream. Now if that's not an obligation to get busy and live your dream, I don't know what is.

When you receive a beautiful, expensive gift, don't you feel obligated to say thank you? Aren't you obligated to make good and valuable use of that gift? Yes! Well, you have received the most valuable gift there is—the gift of your life in this universe of limitless possibilities. So aren't you obligated to say thank you? Aren't you obligated to say thank you by making the very most of that incredibly, unspeakably valuable gift? Reach deep within yourself and connect with the things that are truly important to you, the things you know are you, the things you deeply desire, the values you simply cannot live without, the desires that won't leave you alone. Feel the profound obligation to keep yourself solidly connected with those desires, and to find new, unique and creative ways to express them. Take stock of the great energy and resources and abundance in which you find yourself immersed, and make the choice to make something new, beautiful and magnificent out of it.

Indeed, you're obligated to all of life, and that is also an obligation to yourself. From your perspective, you're the focal point of everything that is. You're the way that all of creation can see and experience and understand itself from a unique and beautiful perspective. You owe it to everything there is to dream real, true, sincere and authentic dreams, and to bring those dreams completely and joyfully to life.

My Big Dream

The dreamers are the saviours of the world. As the visible world is sustained by the invisible, so men, through all their trials and sins and sordid vocations, are nourished by the beautiful visions of their solitary dreamers.

— James Allen

I dream of a world where we all dream, and live our dreams. It is a world in which we don't have to live in fear, of ourselves or of others. I dream of a world that values excellence, a world of meaningful substance. In the world of my dreams, people everywhere appreciate the freedom they have to make a difference, and we each make the most of that opportunity. I dream of a world in which authentic quality is highly valued, a world where we each keep our word, where we understand how honesty and integrity can profoundly add to the quality and value of life.

I dream of a world where we truly appreciate the miracle of existence, the miracle of awareness, the miracle of being able to reason and understand, where we treasure the miracle of being able to love. It is a world that values the mysteries of life, and the fact that there are some things we simply cannot know. In the world of my dreams, all people have faith in the things they can feel and know but cannot explain. I dream of living in a world where we greatly value our lives, and make the most out of every moment, where every person values the very moment he or she is in, and doesn't complain about what has already been, or worry about what might or might not be coming.

I dream of a world in which all people are free to fail, because only when we are free to fail are we also free to succeed. It is a world where we are honest with each other, and honest with ourselves. Integrity takes center stage and is valued. Victims receive loving assistance, but are not encouraged to continue seeing themselves as victims. Achievers are celebrated for the contributions they make, and are cheered on as they achieve even more. Children are lovingly taught by example the value of achievement, the value of discipline, the value of persistence, of commitment, of integrity, of honesty, and the value of understanding truth.

The world of which I dream is a world where positive values are valued, where we understand what real value is, a world where we are not constantly distracted by trivial things, a world in which we are focused on substance, and yet a world in which we enjoy ourselves immensely and have fun. It is a world in which we can laugh and celebrate life and smile and trust and do it genuinely. I dream of living in a world that is fueled by dreams, in which we are not afraid of our dreams, in which we are not ashamed of our dreams, a world where we value those impulses that are deep within us, those purposes that cannot be explained in words, but which inspire and lead to valuable ideas and passions and opinions.

In the world of my dreams, no person is ashamed of following his or her authentic purpose. We live freely and without guilt, unashamed of who we are. We are not scolded for being who we truly are, but rather are encouraged, not to run wild over everyone else, but to be who we are while still respecting the rights of others to be who they are. It is a world in which we can follow our own unique impulses, and yet temper those impulses so they don't interfere with or harm the lives of others.

It is a world in which the self-interest of each person is easily and naturally harnessed so as to lift up everyone. We don't have to be scolded into respecting the common good. Rather, we understand that by following our own interests with integrity, discipline, discretion and consideration for others, we can contribute magnificently and powerfully to the well being of everyone. It is a world of true diversity where each person is celebrated as a unique individual, not as a member of some oppressed or oppressive group, but as a member of a group of one, a unique and beautiful minority of one, with his or her own contributions, with his or her own passions, with his or her own specific, unique opinions, and with his or her own valuable, individual perspective. In the world of my dreams, all of those diverse opinions and passions and perspectives

The Power of Ten Billion Dreams

come together in a respectful way and grow stronger as a result. Diverse positive passions can bounce off of each other and feed on each other and contribute to each other and learn from each other, to all grow stronger, to all grow more life-affirming.

I dream of a world where we can each be secure in owning the fruits of our labor, and don't have to worry about it being confiscated by those who resent us or by those who seek to gain power over us. Every person understands the value of private property and understands the value of protecting private property. Each person understands how when people are free to achieve for their own sake, the value they create lifts up the whole world and benefits everyone. I dream of a world in which we all understand and live according to this simple concept.

It is a world where we celebrate our feelings and emotions and passions, and yet are not held prisoner by them, a world in which we can think and act rationally while living the full magnificence of our emotions. I dream of a world where those who seek to take advantage of others are quickly stopped by the incongruities between their misguided efforts and the values of society at large. It is a world that doesn't need a lot of laws and rules and regulations because the vast majority of people understand that it's never in their best interest to take advantage of anyone else, so there is no need to anticipate and spell out and outlaw all the different possible ways in which people might conceivably take advantage of other people.

The world I dream of is a world where we are each smart enough to take responsibility. We understand that we are each responsible for making our own way in life and that we are responsible for not harming other people. There is widespread understanding and consideration for the fact that we're all in this together. It is a world in which we think of the consequences before we act. We consider the consequences for ourselves and for others. It is a world where we avoid doing things that might harm others while at the same time fully living the beautiful purpose that is within each of us, fully living our own dreams, fulfilling those deepest desires we have, while also respecting and having consideration for other people, and for their dreams.

That's the world I dream of. I know such a world exists already for many people, for more people than most of us realize. But what I dream of is a world in which that kind of world is widely and publicly celebrated, by everyone. A world in which personal responsibility is promoted and encouraged, not only in secret and in private, but publicly by business and government and community leaders. It is a world where we shout from the rooftops the value of responsibility, the value of achievement, the value of effort, the value of making a difference, and the value of living our authentic dreams.

I dream of a world in which our leaders are true leaders—people who lead by example, not by decree. It is a world where people rise to positions of leadership not to gain undue advantage, but because they understand the immense value of the human spirit, because they understand the immense value of individual effort, and the value of individuals all working together and respecting each other.

I dream of a world with leaders who understand the value of individual achievement, the value of incentive, the value of the opportunity to fail and the opportunity to succeed. It is a world where leaders have utmost respect for, and deference to, those they lead, where leaders respect the intelligence of the people they lead. It is a world where leaders become leaders because they have already created great achievements in their own lives, and are therefore are able to inspire by positive example, by encouraging, by respecting, by expecting the very best of those they lead.

It is a world where our institutions do not create slavish dependence by handing out life's necessities and goodies for free, but rather enable people to achieve by ensuring and protecting access to raw opportunity.

I dream of a world in which there is transparency, a world in which we are honest with each other, a world in which our technology serves to open windows on what we do rather than enabling us to hide who we truly are. It is a world where we understand the value of paying the price for the things we get. We value the opportunity to work for what we have, and understand that the real value of anything comes in bringing it about. We also understand that the real value of any possession comes from what is put into it. It is a world where we celebrate the value of effort, where we fully experience that the value of the journey is in making the journey, that the value of the achievement is in creating the achievement, and that there are no shortcuts. I dream of living in a world where we don't waste a lot of time and effort and hopes and dreams on trying to get a big windfall without making any effort, a world in which there's not a lot of effort wasted on trying to avoid effort.

Truly, it is a world where effort and achievement are celebrated. Because achievement is what we do. Achievement is what we're built for. Achievement is what fulfills us. Having things, getting things, getting stuff, that doesn't fulfill us. That never will fulfill us. The stuff is nice. The stuff is powerful. The stuff can be very useful. But the stuff only serves to enable us to make a difference. That—making a difference—is what we long to do.

Making a difference is what we're able to do. That's what we're good at doing. We're good at making things happen. We're good at creating. We're good at feeling that ineffable feeling within ourselves and then translating it into an expression in the outside world. That is a big part of the beauty of life. That is a big part of what it means to be alive. We're not machines. We're not programmed to just make a certain kind of widget with our lives. We're each unique. We're each a unique expression of the mysterious magnificence that is existence. We're each aware, aware that we're here. We're aware that we can do all sorts of things. We're aware of our feelings, aware of our individual passions, aware of our purpose.

We feel what it means to be alive, and even though we can't fully express it, that limitation is beautiful in itself. The fact that we cannot fully express what it means to be alive gives us the opportunity to spend our whole lives doing just that—working on expressing what it means to be alive. That is what fulfills us, connecting with the beauty that lives inside of us, that we cannot put an accurate name on, and making it into something tangible that the whole world can see and enjoy.

That's what a dream is. It's the process of going way down

deep inside and feeling your most fundamental purpose, and then looking out around you and wondering, what can I do? What can I do with this beautiful world that I find myself in, what can I do to connect that deepest inner part of me with this world that's all around me? That is what a dream is. That is the world I dream of, a world in which we all understand the value of doing that, of dreaming.

It is a world where we all understand that the dream underlying all dreams can be expressed in billions of different ways. We understand that we can connect with the unique spark of existence and awareness of everything that is, that wholeness that lives deep, deep within us, and do something with it, maybe something that's never been done, in a way that resonates with all of creation. It is the immense beauty of being alive. Each dream is nothing less than that.

And that's the world I dream of. That's my big dream. That's why I do what I do, when it comes down to it, because I dream of that world. We all dream of that world. You dream of that world. You wouldn't express it in the same way I put it. But you dream of that world, too. Because that is the dream that we all share at some level. We share the dream of universal wholeness. We share the dream that life is good. We share the dream that life is beautiful and that existence is worthwhile and that there's some kind of meaning in all this. We share the desire to find that meaning and to express it as best we can, each in our own individual ways. We share the desire to touch that meaning, to draw it out into the open where everyone can see it. We share the desire to live the meaning, to feel the wonderful, sweet fulfillment of being alive and of knowing that we're making a difference, of knowing that we matter, of knowing that life is good and of knowing that the goodness endures, no matter what.

Though there may be problems, and difficulties and obstacles and tragedies, still that goodness endures. The spark deep within us endures, through pain and disease and even death, through tragedy and loss, through difficulty and pain. Through it all, still there is goodness. There is always that spark of goodness that comprises a fundamental part of all existence, and it exists within us.

That is what a dream expresses. That is what the value of a dream is. And that is why dreams matter. As frivolous as they may sometimes seem, that is why each and every dream matters. And that is why they all can provide immense value.

I dream of a world in which dreams take center stage. I dream of a world in which we are all driven by our dreams, not by our fears, not by our misplaced desires to dominate other people, but driven by the desire to each express our own unique essence.

I dream of a world that is driven by dreams. Will you join me in that world?

16235526R00109

Made in the USA
Lexington, KY
12 July 2012